The Many Faces of Dependency in Old Age

DATE DUE

D1380706

THE MANY FACES OF DEPENDENCY IN OLD AGE

Margret M. Baltes
Free University Berlin

CAMBRIDGE
UNIVERSITY PRESS

Published by the Press Syndicate of the University of Cambridge
The Pitt Building, Trumpington Street, Cambridge CB2 1RP
40 West 20th Street, New York, NY 10011-4211, USA
10 Stamford Road, Oakleigh, Melbourne 3166, Australia

First published 1996

Printed in the United States of America

Library of Congress Cataloging-in-Publication Data
Baltes, Margret M.
The many faces of dependency in old age / Margret M. Baltes.
p.   cm.
Includes bibliographical references and index.
ISBN 0-521-49684-5 (hbk.). – ISBN 0-521-49804-X (pbk.)
1. Aged – Psychology.   2. Aged – Care – Psychological aspects.
3. Dependency (Psychology) in old age.   I. Title.
HQ1061.B35   1996
305.26 – dc20   96-13989
                                                            CIP

A catalog record for this book is available from the British Library.

ISBN 0-521-49684-5 hardback
ISBN 0-521-49804-X paperback

To My Parents

Contents

Contents

Figures and Tables

Preface

This book evolved slowly over the last five years as I started to put together the diverse studies and writings that had emerged from my research program on dependency over the last 20 years. By dependency I mean a characteristic of individual behavior, such as being passive, accepting help, asking for help. It is immediately obvious that this type of dependency, which I have labeled behavioral dependency, is but one among the many types of dependencies in old age, the most prominent of which are structured and physical dependency.

Although the meaning of dependency in the research program has not changed during the long gestation period of the book, its functions have broadened over the years from signifying merely loss to include gains as well.

In the early 1970s as a young assistant professor grounded firmly in social learning theory and a transactional view of dependency, I viewed dependency as the negative outcome of social forces that needed to be changed to allow elderly people to age independently. Consequently, I emphasized the responsibility to create autonomy-enhancing ecologies in old age and to intervene whenever dependency was in sight. I was very slow in recognizing the positive potentials of dependency.

In old age with its diverse losses, dependency, although possibly hastening decline, might be an optimizing strategy in that it initiates and secures social contact. Moreover, dependency might have a compensatory function in that it allows the elderly to conserve energy and, therefore, to engage in more desirable activities. Losses that come with aging are real and often not under the control of us humans. And although some losses are repairable to a degree, there are clear limits to their repair. The elderly person as well as support persons walk a tightrope asking or giving only as much support as necessary, considering the competence level and the losses of the elderly person, or the preferences and motivations of the elderly person.

In this sense, when dependency is the result of social forces regardless of the actual competence level of the elderly, intervention toward independence is warranted; in contrast, when dependency is self-selected in the attempt to compensate for losses due to aging, any intervention effort should better be abandoned. As a product, the book reflects these diverse views of dependency in old age.

This broadening of my thinking about the functions of behavioral dependency was helped along by two theoretical perspectives. There was the life-span perspective that I adopted with Susan Silverberg when examining dependency across the life course and recognizing the dialectic dynamic between independence and dependence at any life stage. There was the gain–loss perspective of aging that was at the core of Paul Baltes's deliberations on life-span psychology and that was responsible for our working together on a metamodel of successful aging.

Of course I was not alone during this long journey since 1975 and I am indebted to a great number of people. There are foremost the students and colleagues. Of the many, I want to give special thanks to Robert L. Burgess and Hans-Werner Wahl; the former for introducing me to the practical and technical know-how of observational research back at Pennsylvania State University, the latter for being the most cooperative, dependable, and supportive research associate in Berlin.

Among the many who have influenced my thinking during this long research program, I would like to mention Al Bandura, Laura Carstensen, Martin Seligman, and above all Paul Baltes. From their respective research agendas, be it self-efficacy, socio-emotional selectivity, learned helplessness, or life-span psychology and successful aging, there came many inputs and stimulations.

I am grateful to the diverse funding agencies. The support of the NIMH, specifically its nursing research section, helped to launch the research program on a wider scale than was previously possible with the seed money from Pennsylvania State University, my professional affiliation during the first years of the research program. The Volkswagen Stiftung then very daringly supported the continuation of my research program in Germany from 1980 to 1986, when I was a newcomer to the German world of science and the Free University of Berlin. The last but very critical phase of the research program, from 1986 till 1990, was made possible by the funding from the then German Ministry for Technology and Research. After all that time and financial and intellectual support, I am able to paint a more complete picture of the conditions and functions of behavioral dependency.

I am also very much indebted to the Psychology Department of Stanford University where I stayed from 1990 to 1991 with a research stipend from the Volkswagen Stiftung to write this book. Polishing the first version went more slowly than expected, and during a second stay at Stanford in 1994 it was ready to be sent off to a publisher. I would like to thank John R. Nesselroade and Hans-Werner Wahl as well as the anonymous reviewer for Cambridge University Press and its editor, Julia Hough, for helpful suggestions on that first version. I have tried to meet the points they raised in their reviews. I hope they will be pleased by the revised manuscript, though whatever shortcomings remain are entirely my responsibility.

Special compliments and thanks are due to Anne Tschida, who did the first editorial job and to Angela Dietl, who sorted and matched all the figures and tables and assisted in preparing the indexes. My staff at the Research Unit of Psychological Gerontology in the Department of Gerontopsychiatry, Jutta Urban and Monika Kleinitz, provided the necessary secretarial support with dedication and the utmost care.

The ultimate expression of gratitude must go to the hundreds of people who gave their time and thoughts as participants in the several studies. With their help, I hope this book will have some positive impact on the lives of future elderly people.

1

Introduction

Aging has long intrigued philosophers and artists. Over the last years scientists, too, have taken an interest in aging and attempted to answer the question: What is aging? The answer is far from conclusive or comprehensive.

As the proportion of the elderly in the population continues to grow, so do the corresponding personal and societal problems. At the same time, previously ignored or unknown potentials and possibilities in old age have become better understood.

One of the most pressing problems of old age is dependency, to a large part considered a necessary part of aging. Dependency, like many other phenomena of aging, is seen primarily as a product of decline and deterioration, as a loss in both physical and mental functioning. Like dependency in childhood, which is seen as a natural step in human development, so too is dependency in later life considered an inevitable consequence of growing old.

In my own research on dependency in old age, I have attempted to overcome this unifunctional, deterministic conception of dependency and have, instead, embraced a multifunctional, contextual, and interactive perspective. This allowed me to demonstrate that dependency due to decline in old age is in large part the outcome of society's negative attitudes toward old age. It is more a self-fulfilling prophecy than a reflection of the true competence level of the elderly. Thus, the research upon which this book is based grew out of my awareness of environmental forces, attitudes, and expectations that might impose dependencies on the aging population. The empirical findings that I report in this book speak for such socially induced dependency.

In the process of this research I became aware also that dependency has more than negative functions and may indeed be highly adaptive, thus representing not only loss but gain. At the end of the book, I expand on this idea when I discuss dependency that may be selected by the person himself or herself. When the elderly become aware of restrictions both in their own capacity and in environmental opportunities, they invariably resort to selection and compensation. In order to maintain and optimize functioning, dependencies in some domains have to be reckoned with.

Thus, the balance in old age between security and autonomy seems highly precarious and might require great investments from society in order to make it work, for example by providing age-friendly environments to protect as well as stimulate personal growth until the end. But this environmental restructuring cannot stand alone. The elderly person, too, is asked to take an active role in the design of his or her aging by accumulating resources, anticipating and realizing losses, and wisely applying the resources for maintenance and optimization of functioning.

The primary intent of this book is to paint a picture of the diversity and complexity of what is hidden behind the term *dependency*. I discuss first the two most widely known dependencies, structured and physical dependency, and then zero in on behavioral dependency.

Structured dependency, has been and still is the focus of research by social demographers and sociologists. This is dependency created by the social structures in our society. The following vignette describes this type of dependency.

Mary, age 72, had been a committed teacher and homemaker all her adult life. She had looked forward to retirement so she could enjoy her major hobbies: reading and golfing. Upon retirement, she did enroll in a reading club and a golf club and her days revolved around these hobbies. Much planning, execution, and enjoyment went into all kinds of activities relating to her hobbies. She also took great pride in keeping up her garden and spent many days digging and planting. Then Mary broke her hip, an injury from which she recovered very slowly. Her ability and strength in motor activities was greatly hampered. She was released from the hospital to her husband's care. She did not want him to be responsible for her care. She wanted to enlist some social services, but it was very difficult for her to get only those services that she desired and thought necessary. Services came in packages. The social worker indicated that, since one never knew what services were actually going to be needed, it was best to take them all. Such oversupply created dependencies that were not based on real need.

Physical dependency is referred to by epidemiologists and is considered to be caused by disease in old age. It has found wide clinical relevance in the construction of Activities of Daily Living (ADL) scales that are used to make decisions about the ability to live independently in the community. Nina in the following vignette exemplifies physical dependency.

Nina, age 72, like Mary, had been a committed teacher and homemaker all her adult life. She had looked forward to retirement so she could enjoy her major hobbies: reading and golfing. Upon retirement, she enrolled in a reading club and a golf club and her days revolved around these hobbies. Much planning, execution, and enjoyment went into all kinds of activities relating to her hobbies. She also took great pride in keeping up her garden and spent many days digging and planting. Then Nina broke her hip, an injury from which she recovered very slowly. Her ability and strength in motor activities was greatly hampered. She was released from the hospital to her husband's care. Her recovery did not, however, proceed as planned. She developed pneumonia and showed signs of increasing mental and physical decline. More and more she became dependent in almost every aspect of life. Her husband together with a home health nurse managed to care for her around the clock.

Then there is what I have labeled behavioral dependency, which is often the focus of psychological studies. Behavioral dependency has at least three etiologies. The first is learned helplessness; the second, learned dependency; and the third, selective optimization with compensation. The first two instances of behavioral dependency can be traced to social environmental conditions. The next two vignettes illustrate dependency due to learned helplessness and due to learned dependency.

Linda, age 72, like Mary and Nina, had been a committed teacher and homemaker all her adult life. . . . She was released from the hospital to her husband's care. When she began to feel her usual self, she tried to get back into her former activities. However, she sometimes experienced a sharp pain as the result of her efforts. At the same time, her husband was never satisfied with her efforts and scolded her for not trying harder. She grew more and more frightened and became afraid to try anything. Now she spends most of her days in her rocking chair feeling despondent and too apathetic even to read.

In contrast, there is the case of Ellen.

Ellen, age 72, like the other women, had been a committed teacher and homemaker all her life. . . . She was released from the hospital to her husband's care. Even now, despite the fact that she has fully recovered, her husband keeps on babying her. He continues to assist her during self-care tasks, he watches over her every step, and admonishes her to not overexert herself. He took away her golf clubs because he is afraid she will try to play golf again. He drives her to her reading club and makes sure she is more a listener than a participant.

I compare these two types of behavioral dependency not to show that one is right and the other wrong but rather to emphasize yet more of the diversity that is connoted by the term "dependency."

As you will see in the book, I will outline most succinctly the major role of the environment in producing the type of behavioral dependency represented by the case of Ellen. I describe a research program spanning 20 years that has led to the formulation of the learned-dependency model. My research findings demonstrate that behavioral dependency results from an overly pampering environment, producing what I call the *dependency–support script*. When expected incompetence – not real incompetence – in the elderly turns care into overcare it results in loss of independence due to disuse. Intervention is called for because, without it, deterioration might be hastened. I will show that environments can be changed to promote an *independence–support script*.

At the same time, I want to emphasize, however, that behavioral dependency may well serve the elderly as an instrument of proxy control. In the end of the book, I, therefore, introduce yet another type of behavioral dependency, behavioral dependency that is self-induced or self-selected and is an integral part of successful aging. There is a type of behavioral dependency that results from coping with the unavoidable shrinking of reserves and capacities in old age. Uncontrollable losses can only be coped with successfully when the elderly person acknowledges such losses and uses compensatory and selection strategies to maintain and perhaps even optimize functioning. The case of Sue gives an example.

> Sue, age 72, had been a committed teacher and homemaker all her life. . . . She was released from the hospital to her husband's care. Even now, despite the fact that she is actually able to get around as usual, she lets herself be assisted by her husband in some of her daily self-care activities (bathing, dressing, grooming). She is no longer doing any gardening or housework. She has, however, resumed golf and is reading even more avidly than before.

Thus, for intervention an analysis of the etiology of dependency seems crucial. With this book, I hope to explicate that dependency in old age has many faces, different etiologies, functions, and consequences, and that the social environment plays a prominent role in its emergence and maintenance.

Specifically, I want to address the questions of how behavioral dependency comes about, how it is maintained, and how it can be changed. The empirical research exemplifies these questions, analyzing social environmental conditions surrounding behavioral dependency.

Why focus on behavioral dependency? This may seem, in some ways, somewhat trivial in comparison to structured and physical dependency. My preference for the domain of behavioral dependency is based on three observations. First, behavioral dependency is one of the dependencies most feared by the elderly. Fear of becoming dependent on others for self-care, for instance, is often used by the elderly to justify their own death. Second, it is the kind of dependency that sets the elderly apart from other age groups (except infancy and early childhood) as incompetent according to adult norms. Behavioral dependency is a task for the elderly that needs to be coped with. Third, although we seem to think that institutionalization will not be part of our life – it only befalls 5% of the elderly – we know that among those who reach age 80 this percentage rises to over 30%. This percentage is high enough to make us all stop and think how we would want to be treated in a long-term institution.

A fourth reason, though less prominent in my own mind, is to counteract the psychodynamic approach to dependency which considers behavioral dependency a personality trait (Bornstein, 1992, 1993; Radebold, 1979) – not to prove its proponents wrong but to show that there can be multiple etiologies.

2

What Is Dependency?

It is common knowledge that in Western societies the cultural imperative is on self-reliance and independence. The emphasis is on individualism and autonomy (Sampson, 1985; Spence, 1985). Despite recent criticism from researchers concerned with female development (Gilligan, 1982a,b) or with a more comprehensive perspective of development (Franz & White, 1985), the Western cultural belief system dictates that dependency is something to be outgrown, not to be sanctioned. Such a cultural system must exert a strong negative impact on any person exhibiting dependent behaviors, but must also specify situations or conditions in which dependency is tolerated. A humane culture respects, for instance, illness and disability as reasons to relieve persons of burdens. Unfortunately, such protection often results also in disempowerment and paternalism, consequences at the root of the conflict between dependency and personal control, autonomy, and competence. The following three statements provide examples of this dynamic:

Only by being independent can an American be truly a person, self-respecting, worthy of concern and the esteem of others (p. 59). . . . It should be emphasized that whether a class of people are believed to have "something of value" to exchange in social relationships is largely a matter of cultural definition. . . . If an individual arbitrarily is defined as having "nothing of value" to exchange, then any claim he makes on others is evidence of dependency (p. 67) (Clark, 1969).

In jeder Beziehung liegt eine Abhängigkeit, selbst mit einem Hund. [There is an element of dependency in every relationship, even with a dog.] (Freud, cited by Wortis, 1954, p. 23).

Dependent relationships are not "regressed" to, they persist throughout the life of most people. They are more troublesome in old age, primarily because they are less elaborately disguised, and are expressed in ways that are less acceptable socially than before (Goldfarb, 1969, p. 3).

Theoretical discussions about the why and how of dependency in old age are often associated with two now classic publications. The first, *The Dependencies of Old People,* was edited by Richard Kalish and published in 1969. This volume represents an interdisciplinary collection of contributions by scientists presenting different theoretical views about the concept of dependency. With the exception of Kalish's paper presenting interview findings, the papers are all theoretical elaborations on dependency from a psychiatric, anthropological, medical, sociological, or social-work perspective. The second book, *Dependency and Interdependency in Old Age,* was edited by Joseph Munnichs and William van den Heuvel and published in 1976. Again we find an interdisciplinary collection of authors who focus on the need for both theoretical and empirical clarification of the term "dependency."

In general, gerontological work on dependency has stagnated at a global and correlational level describing the existence of different types of dependencies in the old. From this descriptive research we can deduce two major issues confronting research on dependency in aging. The first issue concerns dependency as a multidimensional, multifunctional, and multicausal concept. The second issue refers to the connotation whereby dependency implies incompetence, whereas independence implies competence.

Three Characteristics of Dependency: Multidimensionality, Multifunctionality, and Multicausality

Dependency is a highly multifaceted construct much like other psychological concepts such as depression, self, personal control, or aggression. Thus it is not surprising to find in the gerontological literature a wide array of dependencies such as structured, mental, physical, economic, social, emotional, cognitive, real, pseudo, or neurotic dependency. In addition, dependency can be analyzed at many different levels, at the behavioral, personal, situational, or interpersonal level, depending upon one's theoretical and methodological approach. Thus, any approach will most likely concentrate only on specific aspects of dependency and rarely – perhaps never – on the entire picture of dependency. It also follows that dependencies may be interconnected or may occur independently of each other. For example, a person might be physically dependent with or without exhibiting psychological dependencies.

A second issue pertains to the multifunctionality of dependency. In general, dependency appears to be undesirable in Western societies. However, there are variations on this theme not only across different cultures but also within Western cultures. Certain dependencies are not only tolerated but accepted by society for certain individuals at certain times or occasions, for example during illness or mourning, or in young children, where the goal is to increase competence and subsequently more independence. In this vein, it is argued by some authors (e.g., Clark, 1969) that there are some periods or occasions during one's life course in which dependent behaviors are judged to be necessary either as a state of transition toward better health or as a typical expectation of a stage in life. Goldfarb (1969) underlines this notion when maintaining that a successful "therapist–client" relationship is only possible on the basis of dependency of the client. Freud, in the statement quoted earlier as well as in other writings, broadens this view of dependency even further and speaks about the interdependency that is necessary for social relationships in general. Research in the area of adolescent and adult development has come to value interdependence (Baltes & Silverberg, 1994), arguing that both intimacy and generativity can be accomplished only if a person has a high level of both autonomy and interdependency. Thus, we need to examine under which conditions certain aspects of dependency in old age are judged to be functional and even desirable.

Third, dependency is a phenomenon not only of old age but of all life stages. Thus, dependency cannot be associated merely with biological status, but is influenced strongly by social-environmental conditions as well (multicausality). Social, cultural, economical, and psychological factors are acknowledged as operative in the development and maintenance of dependency. Physical frailty (Bortz, 1993) can be a major reason for dependency, though in itself is not automatically a concomitant of aging. Sensory deficits, physical illness, and chronic disease can all be the source of dependency (i.e., Laforge, Spector, & Sternberg, 1992). Medication use and its adverse effects as well as interactions among drugs can be at the root of dependency (Callahan, 1992). Psychoanalytically oriented scholars are interested in determining early developmental roots of dependent personality traits and their association with physical and mental health disorders (Bornstein, 1992, 1993; Greenberg & Bornstein, 1988a,b). Last but not least are physical and social environmental conditions responsible for dependency (Czaja, Weber, & Nair, 1993, Fisher & Carstensen, 1990; Hussian & Brown, 1987; Moos & Lembke, 1985).

Thus, because of the fabric of Western society with its differential economic and social structure, certain groups (e.g., the elderly, women, the unemployed, the handicapped) are more readily labeled dependent than others. In other societal systems with different values, expectations, and goals, the elderly might remain powerful for economic or other social reasons (for instance, if experience and wisdom are highly valued) and not be labeled dependent as easily despite biological decline. In this vein, Clark (1969) speaks of the arbitrariness of the cultural definition of who is dependent when, where, and why.

Silverberg and I (Baltes & Silverberg, 1994) argue that developmental tasks at any life stage affect the dynamic interplay between autonomy and dependency. Certain developmental tasks, like intimacy or generativity, put more emphasis on dependency, whereas other developmental tasks like identity or ego-integrity lean heavily on autonomy. Thus, according to a life-span view of development with developmental tasks as sources for growth, development does not mean growing from dependent to independent, but rather balancing dependency and independence and relying on agency when needed or connectedness when asked for. Such a view allows us to take a more positive view toward dependency and avoid the problem of incompetence.

Dependency and Incompetence

The association of dependency with incompetence and independence with competence is at the core of the negative evaluation of dependency. The association between dependency and incompetence might hold true for early childhood. With special groups such as the mentally retarded and the handicapped, it is of utmost importance to restrict assumptions about incompetence to the very domain of dependency, that is, the need for assistance. All too often, however, domain-specific dependencies, such as physical dependencies, are equated with decisional dependencies and thus total incompetence (Collopy, 1988, 1990). This alignment has catastrophic consequences, since it justifies taking over the lives of people thus deemed incompetent and denying them freedom, choice, and privacy. This same kind of paternalism often applies to the elderly, particularly those in long-term care institutions. Here, control over many aspects of an individual's life, whether or not it is needed or wanted by the resident, is pervasive. Basic rights, such as control over personal property, over one's own body, over one's decision to come and go freely, over access to information and due process, are not often established in long-term care institutions.

Aside from the need to curtail the association of dependency with incompetence, there are kinds of dependencies that should not be associated with incompetence at all. Gilligan (1982a,b) speaks of intimate relationships as being dependent, meaning having an effect on a partner as well as the partner on oneself. Such dependence does not imply being helpless or powerless. Taking care and being cared for empowers both the person and the partner. Interdependence, instead of dependency, has been used to describe this type of behavior.

Furthermore, in the case of dependency as an outcome of a conscious or unconscious effort on the part of a person to yield control to somebody else in a specific domain of life, the association between dependency and incompetence is also questionable. In order to be able to pursue other domains of life higher in priority and perhaps more in line with one's competencies and environmental resources, the elderly might ask somebody else, for instance a son or daughter, to take over in a certain domain of life, say, financial affairs. Here, a felt or expected loss and the ensuing incompetence might provoke a person to select the help of others in a specified domain and thereby compensate for his or her own deficiencies in order to optimize and maintain functioning.

In conclusion, these varieties of dependency highlight the need to focus on analyses that allow us to identify conditions, on both the macro- and the microlevel, that foster and maintain dependency in the elderly. Only then can we sort out the type of dependency with which we are dealing.

The main questions seem to be: Is it true that dependency is a necessary and inevitable corollary of old age? How widespread is the problem of behavioral dependency? How important is the role dependency plays in old age? In attempting to answer these questions, it seems worthwhile to look first at dependency as a socioeconomic and epidemiologic concept to provide a frame for the psychological view and the discussion on behavioral dependency.

Dependency: A Socioeconomic Concept

A major issue with regard to dependency relates to financial and economic dependencies, and economists and sociologists have coined the term "structured" or "social" dependency to address them.

Structured Dependency (the Case of Mary)

The intellectual origins of ideas of structured dependency lie in functionalist social control theories. As a term it implies that human worth is determined primarily by participation in the productive process. Loss of work or retirement creates structured dependency (Townsend, 1981; Walker, 1980). Thus, in essence, culture lays the groundwork for dependency, and its societal structure even requires dependency from certain subgroups in the population in order to function. Although this position has been rebutted (Johnson, 1989), it has stood its ground and is used, for instance, in the determination of the dependency ratio.

Dependency Ratio

In searching for an estimate of the magnitude of dependency in old age, the term "dependency ratio" will most likely be encountered. This term has been coined by demographers to represent the relative productivity of persons forming the age structure of a society and its implications for societal functioning (for a full discussion, see Hauser, 1976). The dependency ratio reflects the proportion of the working population who are supposedly available to support those who are not in the labor force. Commonly, the dependency ratio relates to the number of people who are unproductive because of age (under 15 and over 65 years of age), because of infirmity, or because they are involved in an organized activity such as child rearing, to those who are productive, usually employers or employees between the ages of 15 and 65. This ratio – often labeled macrodependency (Matras, 1989) – is crucial data for social planning, because it indicates the locations along the age spectrum at which there are more dependents than working producers. Social planning takes different directions depending on whether the dependents are mostly young or mostly old.

Statistics show that dependency ratios are increasing in Western cultures relative to the increase of elderly in the population. It is interesting to note that this, in turn, is due to general improvements in the standard of living and the corresponding higher life expectancies for the population.

It is obvious that in the context of dependency ratios, dependency is defined solely on the grounds of being out of the labor force or unproductive with regard to actual participation in the regime of material production. No information is as yet provided about the specific needs or dependencies of people, such as the elderly, who are out of the labor force and might require environmental change to yield the resources for prolonged autonomy. Nevertheless, information about such dependency ratios has alerted researchers, practitioners, and politicians to the necessity for inquiry into the needs and dependencies of the elderly population. Never before has there been as much emphasis on social services for the elderly, at least in European countries. Most are aimed at maintaining independence or independent living and at avoiding institutionalization.

But the design of these services has not taken into account the large interindividual variation among the elderly (P. B. Baltes, 1987). In fact, Guillemard (1992) argues that the designers have missed the goal altogether. She maintains that because of the fragmentation of these services, the elderly person becomes highly dependent upon a service system and once in the system cannot escape leading to structured dependency. This situation is described in the case of Mary.

In sum, the economic factor has been considered the most frequent social or extrinsic cause for dependency in old age. When such economic dependency exists, be it with regard to the elderly, handicapped, or mentally retarded adult, the poor, or the prisoner, the state or social services or relatives assume the posture of parents. Those who manage these social services and provide assistance or care (e.g., nursing homes), come to enjoy a degree of control and power over their clients that normally only parents hold over their minor children. Elderly people needing support for daily sustenance share much with children, mental patients, and even prisoners. This kind of paternalism is allowed because it is assumed that it is in the interest of the client.

In contrast to macrodependency is the condition Matras (1989) labels microdependency, which refers to dependencies in daily living that require assistance. The latter may include being dressed, having meals prepared, having arrangements made for transportation, or having one's bank affairs taken care of. Microdependency, to which we turn now, has been a domain of interest, on the one hand, of epidemiologists and demographers who want to define specific needs of the elderly population; and on the other hand, of psychologists who are interested in uncovering the underlying processes of dependency.

Dependency: An Epidemiological Concept

Another major issue with regard to dependency concerns health problems, organic and mental illnesses, as well as impairment. Demographers and epidemiologists have long been interested in counting the proportion of the population that is physically or funtionally dependent.

Physical Dependency (the Case of Nina)

Among those who live in the general community, it is estimated that between 5% and 8% of persons over the age of 65 show dependencies in some domains of self-care or household care (Guralnik & Simonsick, 1993; see Sosna & Wahl, 1983; Wahl, 1993). Obviously this situation reflects the case of Nina, described earlier, whose physical problems make it increasingly difficult for her to remain independent. We know that a strong correlation exists between age and physical dependency. About 5% of old people live in long-term care institutions (Brock, Guralnik, & Brody, 1990; Linden, Gilberg, Horgas, & Steinhagen-Thiessen, in press). This rather low estimate is based on cross-sectional and one-shot studies. The likelihood that a given individual in his or her lifetime will be in an institution is judged to be much higher, but any given estimate is a rough one, as it would require cohort-longitudinal studies (P. B. Baltes, Reese, & Nesselroade, 1977). The lifetime risk of institutionalization is roughly estimated as 25% (Bickel & Jaeger, 1986; Kastenbaum & Candy, 1973). In addition, the likelihood of using nursing homes increases with age, with 22% of those over the age of 85 and over 30% of those 95 and older residing in long-term care facilities (Hing, 1987; Linden et al., in press).

In any case, it is generally assumed that institutionalization is preceded by increasing dependency and the need for support and help (Baltes, Wahl, & Reichert, 1991). According to recent data from the 1987 U.S. National Medical Expenditure Survey (NMES) (Lair & Lefkowitz, 1990), more than half of elderly nursing home residents had difficulties in four or more domains of functioning. Some social scientists, like Maddox (1984), argue that about 40% of the institutionalized elderly could manage at home given adequate resources for independent living. A similar conclusion is drawn by Bortz (1989, 1993), who promotes the notion that much of frailty is a consequence of disuse, or in my own argument, detailed later in this book, that shows that much of dependency is a consequence of social environmental conditions.

To evaluate epidemiological work on dependency we need to know how physical dependency is defined and how it is measured.

In epidemiological studies the term dependency is defined pragmatically as "functional incapacity" (e.g., Shanas et al., 1968; Wan, Odell, & Lewis, 1982) or as "practical helplessness" (van den Heuvel, 1976). The basic position of epidemiological research on dependency is perhaps best characterized by the following statement: "Another extremely important factor related to adjustment is the individual's capacity to carry out the essential activities of daily living" (Gallagher, Thompson, & Levy, 1980, p. 30). In some epidemiological studies we find an attempt to differentiate between dependency and disability. In this sense, Akhtar, Broe, Crombie, McLean, & Andrews (1973), for instance, restrict dependency to problems in personal maintenance activities.

In addition to such differentiations and similar ones, there is the "International Classification of Impairments, Disabilities, and Handicaps" (ICIDH), published by the World Health Organization (WHO) in 1980. This classification scheme represents a strong association between disease, impairment, and disability on the one hand, and (a separate term) "handicap" as the role-impairing result of disability, on the other. The catalogue of dependencies accompanying this classification scheme contains, aside from activities of daily living, dysfunctions in communication, orientation, and cognitive performances. It is obvious that estimates of numbers or percentages of dependent persons will depend on the measurement used.

Despite these differences in the definition of physical dependency, there exists general agreement on activities relevant to dependency that most epidemiological studies attempt to assess, namely the areas of self-maintenance, home-maintenance, mobility, and impairment in hearing and vision. There remain, however, differences as to the rating procedure of independence/dependence.

In comparing a number of studies, the ratings range from a very global estimate to a scoring system differentiating among domains of daily activities including self-care and instrumental activities such as using the telephone, shopping, managing medications, and so on. The most commonly used instruments to measure physical dependency are the Activities of Daily Living (ADL) scale (Katz, Ford, Moskowitz, Jackson, & Jaffe, 1963) or the scale

Instrumental Activities of Daily Living (IADL) (Lawton & Brody, 1969). If one looks only at ADL activities and domains, the dependencies remain quite low, at least until the age of 85.

In most assessment instruments, dependency is rated on a three-point scale: (1) activities that can be executed without help or special efforts, (2) activities that can only be executed when special efforts are made by the individual, and (3) activities that are executed with the help of others. In this rating procedure either a global estimate for one entire domain, such as self-care, is made, or each subarea within one domain, such as bathing or grooming, is rated and those ratings are added to form an overall score. An arbitrary cutoff point is often used to differentiate between independence and dependence. Efforts toward the development of Guttman-like scales (e.g., Sandholzer, 1982) have improved the precision of measurement and predictability of degree of dependency – provided certain prerequisites such as satisfactory coefficients of reproducibility and scalability are met. They have also improved comparability of both future large-scale studies and diagnostic procedures in applied settings. There is no instrument yet that could be applied to a representative sample of old people. Given the differences in the definition and the assessment of dependencies discussed above, it is not surprising that the findings are equivocal and thus should be taken only as rough guidelines.

No wonder, then, that prevalence rates vary. When only those old people who need actual and regular help in self-care tasks are considered, the percentages are very low. Such findings support the statement by Maddox (1984, p. 22) that "the risk of impairment and dependency in later life should not be exaggerated." When expanding the definition of dependency to include those elderly who need actual and regular help in both self-care and instrumental daily activities, such as household tasks, the percentages increase drastically. For instance, Cooper (1984) reports every second woman over 65 to be somewhat dependent. Similarly, Wan et al. (1982) find that 27.1% of people over 60 need some help in at least one instrumental daily activity. In contrast, Guralnick and Simonsick (1993) and Wahl (1993) report that between 5% and 8% of those over the age of 65 show ADL dependency. One needs to keep in mind that most percentages reported in the literature do include old people needing "potential" as well as "actual" help, thus referring to both the already dependent and those who run the risk of becoming dependent in the near future.

In general, we can conclude that the extent of physical dependence is affected by a number of variables, foremost of which are gender, institutionalization, and age. Thus, physical dependency is higher in women (Baltes et al., in press; Guralnick & Simonsick, 1993; Verbrugge, 1989), in people over 85 (Brock, Guralnick, & Brody, 1990; Zarit, Johansson, & Berg, 1993), and in long-term care residents (Lair & Lefkowitz, 1990). Accordingly, epidemiological findings on dependency need careful scrutiny. More precise knowledge about prevalence rates is direly needed so as to be able to specify dependency-related needs of the elderly and to design optimal environmental conditions for the elderly.

The Bias of Physical Dependency

Epidemiological work on dependency in aging has been limited largely to the presentation of frequencies of dependencies and the report of correlational relationships between dependency and other variables such as age (e.g., Svanborg, Landahl, & Mehlström, 1984), social class, sex (Sosna & Wahl, 1983; Wan et al., 1982), or psychiatric impairment (Wahl, 1987). Although there is no doubt that physical dependency increases with age, this expectation has led to two negative consequences. First, physical dependency is generalized to affect all old people regardless of age, living conditions, and health. Second and much worse, physical dependency is often generalized to the state of the entire person, labeling as mentally incompetent the elderly adult who is unable to take care of his or her own affairs because of a physical dependency.

The point that needs to be highlighted is this: Physical dependency can be a precursor to behavioral dependency if, after the physical need for help is gone, help is not withdrawn but is instead continued. This is at the base of behavioral dependency, as I will argue and outline in the remainder of the book. This requires, however, a move from the purely descriptive level to an explanatory level – that is, to analysis of the conditions of dependency.

Dependency: A Psychological Concept

In order to understand the conditions of dependency and its prevention or correction, we need to know more about the processes underlying dependencies. Let us turn, therefore, to some theoretical efforts in the field of psychology of dependency. What do we know about dependency in different phases of the life cycle?

Dependency in Early Childhood

Dependency as a psychological construct was already a topic of interest in the 1950s in child psychology (Beller, 1957; Hartup, 1963; Heathers, 1953; Sears, Whiting, Nowlis, & Sears, 1953). Explanations varied from dependency as instinct, as promoted by ethological theory (Bowlby, 1969), or dependency as drive, as promoted by psychoanalytic thinking (Freud, 1958), to dependency as learned behavior, as embraced by social learning theorists (Bandura & Walters, 1963; Cairns, 1972; Gewirtz, 1972; Sears, 1972), and dependency as immature cognitive structures (Schaffer & Emerson, 1964). The dominant assumption in these diverse approaches, save for the cognitive developmental one, was that dependency is supported by a basic need, drive, or trait for care, assistance, and warmth.

In these different approaches dependency is considered as a cluster of behaviors: seeking physical contact, seeking to be near others, seeking attention, seeking praise and approval, resisting separation. It is important to note here and to remember when the topic of behavioral dependency in the elderly is again addressed, that two classes of behavior, "seeking help" and "asking questions," are not part of this list. Some authors did include these two response classes only when they related to instances in which the child did not need information or help per se but used them as means of getting "contact."

Similarly, Lois Murphy (1962) made this differentiation in separating help seeking as part of competent coping behavior from help seeking as passive dependency or insecurity. In the former instance, dependency is a response in which the child dominates or controls others; in the latter, it is submissive. So in the first case we would predict no conflict between dependency and autonomy, in the second, conflict is most likely.

Rather early differentiations were made classifying dependency into emotional versus instrumental dependency, and the two were believed to have different developmental histories (Sears, Maccoby, & Levin, 1957). Bandura and Walters (1963) abandoned this distinction and defined dependency as a "class of responses that are capable of eliciting positive attending and ministering responses from others." Other distinctions were made between passive and active dependency (Kagan, 1971) and between secure and insecure attachment (Ainsworth, 1969, 1972).

Most of the empirical research on dependency in infants and nursery school children involved behaviors such as crying, clinging, proximity seeking, and attention seeking. The primary aims of the empirical studies were (1) to demonstrate stability of the phenomena dependency and independence across age or development, and (2) to predict dependency problems in schoolchildren from the behavior patterns of parents, mostly mothers, during earlier times, mostly infancy (Sears et al. 1957; Sears, Rau, & Alpert, 1965; Sears et al. 1953). In general, it can be stated that research findings did not provide persuasive empirical support for these research goals. First, the correlations among the various social behaviors defined as dependency turned out to be only nominal. Second, the attempts to predict from behavior patterns of mothers a later dependency (i.e., in preschool years) proved largely unsuccessful, partly perhaps, because of the correlational nature of most of the research. Observations of or interview data on mother behaviors were correlated with observations of child behaviors. Only very few studies at the time actually recorded everyday interactions between mother and child. Instead of changing the research strategy, however, research on dependency was discarded when the powerful attraction of a new construct appeared on the horizon: the concept of attachment.

The advancement of the concept of attachment (Ainsworth,

1969, 1972; Bowlby, 1969; Maccoby, 1980; Sroufe & Waters, 1977) centered on the positive features of close parent–child relations and the importance of such a relationship for future development. Behaviors indicative of attachment were not to be extinguished; on the contrary, they were to be fostered as one of the ingredients necessary for a healthy development. In hindsight, it seems fair to conclude that the new concept did not bring a magic cure, but rather contributed to the already existing confusion.

The 1980s saw a renewed interest in dependency, and particularly in overdependency, which had remained a cornerstone of clinical work all along. Dependency is no longer linked to a drive or trait model; rather emphasis is put on the structural changes of dependency and on its association with attachment across the life span (Sroufe, Fox, & Pancake, 1983).

Dependency after Early Childhood

Dependency and, specifically, emotional dependency or attachment in infancy and early childhood was seen as a unitary system. It seems reasonable to assume that the very emphasis on studying dependency in this early life stage allowed such a unitary perspective. Research on dependency in later childhood and adolescence seems to require a much more differentiated approach to describe and explain the many different dimensions of dependency (Maccoby & Masters, 1970).

In later life stages there seems to be more conflict and tension between autonomy and dependency, particularly in adolescence and late adulthood (Baltes & Silverberg, 1994). This conflict is perhaps the main psychological topic in the psychology of adolescence (Blos, 1967; Erikson, 1963; Ryan & Lynch, 1989; Steinberg, 1990; Steinberg & Silverberg, 1986). The conflict between dependency and independence is conceptualized as a stage in development in which the dilemma created by the crisis of identity versus a continuing desire for intimacy needs to be resolved (Erikson, 1963). Although modern theoretical experimentation and empirical findings do not support the idea of two opposing forces, striving for autonomy and emotional detachment from parents, the outcome is considered the same (Ryan & Lynch, 1989; Steinberg, 1990). It is assumed that the process of individuation and autonomy, a most pronounced developmental task of adolescence, will find its mature expression in the balance between personal autonomy and social connectedness or interdependence. Interdependence is the goal and the base of mature adulthood and personal adjustment.

Dependency in Old Age

Such a normative developmental course from dependency to interdependence, promising full personal adjustment in adulthood, has been extended to the third phase of life as well. In contrast to the recognition of conflicts between independence and dependence in adolescence and early adulthood, however, no personality theory predicts a conflict between dependency and autonomy in middle or late adulthood, despite the fact that personal competencies and environmental demands change drastically. Parmelee and Lawton (1990) wrote about the dialectic relationship between dependency and autonomy created by the dynamic interplay between changes in personal competence and environmental demands (see also Wahl & Baltes, 1992).

Recognizing one's limits and accomplishments in middle adulthood and focusing on generativity rather than further personal strivings are typical concerns of midlife (see Hunter & Sundel, 1989). Shifting gears from achievement orientation to relationships is not a turn easily taken by many middle agers. Self-realization in old age may be an even more difficult task. Recognizing one's limited reserves and future time, one's finality and increasing impairments is a hard prospect for the elderly. Defining one's own niche in life, or feeling whole about one's life, seems to be a necessary adaptive process in old age. Here too, developmental tasks require dependency, interdependence, and autonomy. Numerous empirical data speak to the preference of old people for "intimacy at a distance," for more weight on personal autonomy rather than reciprocal relationships. Being or becoming a burden to one's children or one's family, on the one hand, or entering an institution, on the other, constitutes one of the greatest fears and most difficult developmental tasks of the elderly. Thus, in old age, personal autonomy seems to loom large as a guarantor for successful coping with the developmental tasks at hand.

I would like to argue, therefore, that dependency and autonomy present a developmental struggle as much for the elderly in their environment as for adolescents in their environment. I propose that to cope with dependency-producing events, to incorporate dependency and accept and adapt to it where and when necessary – and conversely avoid it where unnecessary – is an integral part of successful aging.

I mentioned earlier that dependency in old age, although beset with many of the same problems as dependency in infancy, has attracted much less research and fewer theoretically sophisticated debates and formulations. In fact, most work on dependency in the aged (Blenkner, 1969; Exton-Smith & Evans, 1977; Kalish, 1969; Munnichs & van den Heuvel, 1976) has been carried out independently of the discussions in the field of child development. Gerontological research on dependency, at least within psychology, has stagnated at a purely descriptive, highly global, and correlational level, merely describing the presence of dependence. Dependency in the gerontological literature is defined generally as helplessness or powerlessness in the common sense of the word. Keeping in mind the risk of oversimplification, we can summarize past research on dependency in aging as being biased by the belief that dependency is the result of biological decline and the ensuing loss of control; thus, dependency is considered the norm in old age and valued negatively. This view is reflected in the concept of dependency as the product of physical decline (see physical dependency in epidemiology) as well as in the social breakdown model of Kuypers and Bengtson (1973).

The risk of losing personal autonomy can arise however, not only from intrinsic causes, such as biological decline, but also from extrinsic ones, such as aging stereotypes, or from a combination thereof. Intrinsic causes are often considered necessary corollaries of aging and can lead to physical dependency (see pages 15–18. Many times a physical impairment might be the triggering effect for behavioral dependency. The latter, however, is re-inforced by the environment and thus is an example for dependency caused by external forces.

Certainly, from advanced adulthood on, aging brings with it increased infirmity, impairments, and losses which, in turn, may lead to reliance on others. Nevertheless, the constellation of conditions related to aging seems to vary widely. Some people are dependent at 50, while others are fully independent at 80. Some are dependent when required to cope with their own financial situation, others with loneliness, and yet others with daily self-care. How early or how late we become unable to cope with this or that aspect of our lives seems to depend on differences in biological makeup as well as on differences in the cumulative effect of social and physical life events; for instance, current and previous life-style choices, medical developments, as well as mental health status and cognitive status will have an impact.

Following these considerations, it does not seem useful to consider dependency in the elderly as foremost a universal and irreversible biological decline process. A biological impairment etiology is but one developmental pathway to dependency. Biological impairment is neither a necessary nor a sufficient condition for dependency. Despite this disclaimer, within the dynamics of social interactions and social perception, dependency is frequently interpreted as a sign of general incompetence. In this vein, Collopy (1988) asked the question: Within the dynamics of care, is physical dependency interpreted as a sign of decisional dependency? There seems to be a direct link between competence and autonomy versus incompetence and dependency without any variations in between.

Thus, it seems of utmost importance to analyze and identify the external reasons for dependency. This obvious gap in the mostly descriptive research in dependency in old age brings us conveniently to the major topic in this book, behavioral dependency in old age.

3
Behavioral Dependency in Old Age

In recent years two approaches concentrating on behavioral dependency have shed new light on dependency in the elderly. Both approaches present developmental courses toward behavioral dependency which reflect dependent behaviors as the outcome of previous and ongoing person–environment transactions and as an accumulation of various life events (see for instance P. B. Baltes, Reese, & Lipsitt, 1980, and Brim & Ryff, 1980, for a discussion and categorization of life events from a life-span perspective). A more complete understanding of dependency in the elderly might be achieved when a variety of conditions – intrinsic and extrinsic causes – under which dependency comes about and is maintained, are considered and analyzed.

Two explanatory paradigms – learned helplessness and learned dependency – treat behavioral dependency as an environmentally induced phenomenon. Theoretically, they differ in their specification of the sources for dependency (noncontingency vs. differential contingency) and their evaluation of the resulting outcome (dependency as loss vs. dependency as loss and gain). Practically, they differ in terms of the nature of intervention (whether to intervene and in which direction to intervene).

The following elaboration on the differences of these two models is not intended to persuade the reader that one model is better than the other. Rather, my intent is to show that both models describe and explain different but equally valid etiologies of dependency. Dependency is, indeed, a multifaceted and multicausal concept.

Behavioral Dependency as the Product of Helplessness or Loss of Control (the Case of Linda)

Over the last decade we have witnessed in psychology a growing interest in the importance of autonomy and control for human development across the life span. Examples are the models of self-efficacy (Bandura, 1977; 1982), agency (Kuhl, 1981; 1986; Skinner, 1985; Skinner & Connell, 1986), of personal control (Lefcourt, 1976) or illusion of control (Langer, 1979; 1983), or learned helplessness (Seligman, 1975). Despite the differences in the theoretical focus of these models, ranging from a social-learning to an action-theoretical orientation, the major link between dependency and personal control is assumed to be based on two major cognitions, namely two expectations or beliefs on the part of the individual actor: (1) "I am in command of behaviors or skills producing specific outcomes and consequences that are required by the situation at hand"; and (2) "the world in which I live is a contingent one and I am dealing with a responsive environment."

Seligman (1975) and his collaborators demonstrated that in the case of a lack of systematic, predictable connections between behavioral and environmental events, animals and humans learn that their behaviors have no differential consequences. This situation has been termed by Seligman "noncontingency." Given repeated experience with noncontingency, negative outcomes result, such as cognitive deficits or lack of performance, motivational deficits or passivity, and emotional deficits or depressivity. Later "cognitive reformulations" of the original model added attributional perspectives (Abramson, Seligman, & Teasdale, 1978). A person will perceive this lack of behavioral consequences as failure and attribute it to either personal incompetence or to an unresponsive environment, or both. Depending on one's attributional style, noncontingency is believed to lead to the experience of lack of control and, in turn, to learned helplessness and dependency. In sum, the major focus of dependency as learned helplessness is its occurrence in noncontingent environments and the conclusion that the resulting outcome is dysfunctional, that is, a type of loss. The case of Linda illustrates this situation. However hard Linda tries, she is nevertheless scolded by her husband for not trying hard enough, and the result is her withdrawal, passivity, and dependency (see page 3).

More recent elaborations of control models have qualified this association between dependency and loss of control by introducing finer differentiations between, for instance, primary and secondary control (Heckhausen & Schulz, 1993; Rothbaum, Weisz, & Snyder, 1982; Schulz, 1986; Schulz, Heckhausen, & Locher, 1992), assimilative and accommodative coping (Brandtstädter & Renner, 1990; Brandtstädter, Wentura, & Greve, 1993), or between primary and proxy control (Bandura, 1982). By distinguishing between primary and secondary control or between assimilative and accommodative coping, the elderly person is aware that in the face of irreversible and irrevocable events, losses are inevitable. Successful coping can no longer be achieved by changing the environment (assimilative coping or primary control), that is patching up the loss, but by accepting the loss and changing one's goals or desires (accommodative coping and secondary control). It should be noted here that Azuma's (1984) critique concerning the need for greater differentiation within the concept of secondary control does not deter from the preceding argument.

By the term *proxy control,* the assumption is made that in the case of loss of competencies and subsequent dependencies, the competencies can be compensated for by delegating primary control. The individual defers his or her primary control to somebody else and thereby stays in control of events.

This thinking comes very close to the explanation of behavioral dependency as being the product of environmental contingencies, in contrast to the product of noncontingencies. My own empirical work (described below) demonstrates that some behavioral dependencies or dependent behaviors are the result of the presence of specific environmental contingencies and personal competencies rather than the presence of noncontingencies and incompetencies. These are situations in which behavioral dependency can be instrumental in maintaining personal control. Dependent behaviors, thus, are not always helpless behaviors. Figure 1 summarizes the major differences in the two models. Let us turn now to behavioral dependency as an instrument of personal, albeit passive, control.

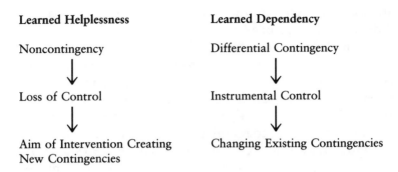

Learned Helplessness	Learned Dependency
Noncontingency	Differential Contingency
↓	↓
Loss of Control	Instrumental Control
↓	↓
Aim of Intervention Creating New Contingencies	Changing Existing Contingencies

Figure 1. Differences between the two models of dependency.

Behavioral Dependency as the Product of Overcare: The Model of Learned Dependency (the Case of Ellen)

Similar to Seligman's original model, the main aspect of my own research on dependency is an account of environmental conditions involved in the maintenance and development of dependent behaviors in old age. In contrast, however, the model of learned dependency assumes the existence of differential environmental contingencies for dependent versus independent behaviors as well as differential or multifunctional outcomes for dependency. Thus, the goal of this research approach is to demonstrate the existence of contingencies rather than their nonexistence. We see the environmental contingency very nicely in the case of Ellen. Despite her newly regained competencies, her husband reacts in an overprotective manner and shields her from doing things herself or exerting herself more than he thinks is advisable.

Similar to the learned-helplessness paradigm (Seligman, 1975), my own research program uses a microanalytic approach to identify social environmental conditions under which dependent and independent behaviors occur or do not occur. To analyze the social environmental system producing behavioral dependency, we employed three convergent methodological strategies (Baer, 1973): an experimental, a sequential observational, and an ecological intervention strategy.

I started out with experimental analyses of behavioral dependency, not in the laboratory with animals, but in natural field situations with elderly persons. Similar to Seligman, my main interest was not in counting how often dependent behaviors occurred, or in comparing the frequency of dependent behaviors between elderly persons and younger age groups, or between elderly with different personality traits or life histories; rather, the question that interested me was whether dependent behaviors of the elderly could be changed, modified, or reversed. The environment (i.e., social partners such as staff members in long-term care institutions), too, was observed and assessed in a contextual, microanalytic manner. Thus, none of the personality or educational characteristics of the staff, the value orientations of the institution or the philosophy of the administration, or the large-scale physical environmental characteristics were manipulated to introduce change in dependent behaviors of the elderly. Instead, immediate reinforcements (praise for holding one's fork; listening to a piece of music after washing one's face) and stimulus control mechanisms (not eating at the table where the "noneaters" were seated) were applied to observe their impact on dependent behaviors of the elderly.

The research project did not stop with the experimental behavioral analysis. It seemed worthwhile and absolutely necessary to extend the analysis and make use of "convergent operations" (Baer, 1973; McCall, 1977) to obtain a more comprehensive understanding of the ecological context of behavioral dependency.

This brought up a second point: What happens in the natural, everyday environment when the elderly exhibit dependent or independent behaviors? This question cannot be answered with experimental analyses but requires systematic, microanalytic observations of naturally occurring streams of behavior. Thus, behavioral sequences between actor and social partner in the everyday life of an institution, for instance, are recorded in their natural occurrence. In Barker's (1968) view, the behavior setting of dependency and independence of the elderly person is described in detail. In addition, however, and going beyond Barker, the naturally occurring behavioral sequences are not only described, but then reconstructed in terms of antecedent–consequent relationships and thus explained within the social-learning framework. Behavioral dependency is studied as a dyadic social phenomenon (person–environment relationship) expressed in concrete behaviors that are regarded as events worth studying in their own right. In other words, such molecular analyses shift our interest away from global constructs (e.g., emotional dependency) to concrete behaviors and their interrelationships, which, in the tradition of child dependency research, are considered indexes of the construct dependency.

Rather than arguing for personality and cognitive processes determining the person–environment relationships, the behavioral approach makes the assumptions that (1) each person is in command of a repertoire of voluntary behaviors or acts; (2) each environment – whether physical, personal, or otherwise – may act as a stimulus, facilitating or hindering the occurrence of behaviors; and (3) each person–environment transaction may present a reinforcing or punishing contingency. That is, each environment sets the stage for certain behaviors to occur and for other behaviors to be avoided. Furthermore, each behavior is followed by either supportive or nonsupportive reactions or is ignored. In a responsive environment, consequences are mostly either reinforcing or punishing. This is not to suggest that the person is a passive pawn or that only the person is acted on by the environment. The perspective of person–environment interactions as contingencies provides for a person's acting on the environment in changing environments or choosing those environments in which behaviors and behavioral goals are stimulated and reinforced.

Combining the concept of behavior setting with a social-learning framework makes it possible to go beyond a mere descriptive classification of observed behaviors and environments (that is, beyond Barker's behavior-mapping strategy) by understanding behaviors and environments as contingencies. This conceptual approach makes it possible to answer such questions as: Why do predictable, regular, and different patterns of behavior occur in different settings? Why do people change their behaviors when they go from one setting to another? What mechanisms exist in settings to keep the behaviors of the occupants within the range acceptable to or desirable by "others" and congruent with the setting's physical features?

Our work does not stop here. It is one thing to show reversibility of behavioral dependency and the existence of typical, interactional patterns fostering behavioral dependency in everyday life of the elderly. It is another to show (1) that these interactional patterns are not merely temporal sequences but functional units and (2) that there are specific belief systems held by old people and their interaction partners concerning these interactions in the context of dependence and independence in old age.

In sum then, our main research questions are

1. Is behavioral dependency modifiable, plastic, or reversible?
2. What are the natural environmental conditions fostering dependent behaviors in the elderly? This question is tied to corollary issues of generalizability of interaction patterns.
3. What explains the behavior of social partners, that is, what are the underlying belief systems?
4. Can we modify these "natural" conditions and, if so, can we thereby produce a change in the interaction patterns?

Answering the first question requires employing an experimental research strategy to clarify the issue of modifiability by examining changes in dependent behavior following changes in environmental conditions. To identify existing behavior–consequence relationships (Question 2), we need sequential observational methodology to capture and analyze naturally occurring behavior sequences between the actors (elderly) and their social partners. To get at belief systems (Question 3) we need to extend our paradigm beyond the observational one and include interview techniques as well as experimental techniques. Finally, the issue of whether the patterns can be changed (Question 4: functional validity of the temporal behavioral sequences) needs to be addressed by using an intervention strategy. Here interventions are designed – based on evidence from experimental and observational work – to change the behavior of the social partners observed in the interactions.

In summary then, the use of the behavioral model for the study of behavioral dependency will (1) inform us about the plasticity of behavioral dependency, (2) provide insight into the natural environmental conditions fostering dependent behaviors in the elderly, and (3) allow us to test whether the observed conditions contingent upon dependent and independent behaviors have functional validity. Behavioral covariation is a necessary but not sufficient condition for inferring causality, and thus the observed system has to be intervened upon to test its causal relationship. The methodological extension to include interview techniques will enrich the data by adding the subjective component, namely knowledge about the belief or attribution system of the elderly and their social partners with regard to independence and dependence.

4

Empirical Research Program on Learned Dependency

Summary of Theoretical and Methodological Framework

The basic goal of our research program has been to identify, describe, and explain the *behavioral social system* of dependency operating in the environment of the elderly. The chief aspect of our research on dependency is an account of environmental conditions involved in the maintenance of dependent behaviors. This is accomplished by a multimethod approach using both experimental research and direct observation of the behavior of the elderly and their partners in the natural environment of institutions and the home, as well as broad-scale intervention research and verbal data.

The research essentially focuses on the question: What is the behavioral system facilitating dependency in old age? The major objective is to demonstrate that *environmental* factors are operating in the development and maintenance of dependency in old age. To meet this objective and answer the question we have to fulfill at least two requirements. For one, a *behavioral level of analysis* has to be selected. This will allow a microanalysis of the behavioral events to which the phenomenon dependency refers. Second, an *interactional level of analysis* has to be chosen, since our interest is not in the frequency of dependent behaviors but in the conditions under which they occur. We chose to focus on dyadic social phenomena, on social environmental conditions, rather than physical environmental conditions of dependent behaviors (e.g., a steep staircase curtailing the person's mobility and making her a prisoner of her apartment). The study of physical environmental conditions as facilitating or hindering factors for independent behavior of the elderly has been taken up by a number of ecological psychologists interested in gerontology (Moos, 1976; Regnier, 1981; Parr, 1980).

Considering these requirements, the social-learning model lends itself rather naturally as a theoretical framework. At the core of the social-learning model is the idea of behavioral analysis looking at person–environment interactions as antecedent and consequent relationships. These relationships, according to behavioral principles, can be reconstructed as reinforcing, punishing, or extinguishing. To examine the interactions with regard to a certain phenomenon, namely behavioral dependency, convergent operations can be brought to bear: an operant experimental research strategy, an operant observational, and an ecological intervention strategy (Baer, 1973).

I should hasten to add here that the selection of any theoretical framework has both benefits and costs. In the case of the social-learning model, specificity and accuracy is bought at the cost of scope. We will be looking at a very small, although important, strand of the global construct dependency, behavioral dependency. Let me summarize, then, the research questions together with the titles of the respective studies that will be the guide in the presentation of the empirical findings.

Four Main Research Questions and Related Studies

Research Question 1: Is dependent behavior in the elderly modifiable? For example, can we change and reverse even chronic dependent behaviors in an elderly person being fed by staff for five years or more? Can an elderly person not having dressed herself for a number of years be taught to do so again? In order to answer these questions we used an experimental design to see whether an elderly person can relearn to eat, dress, or walk independently. Our own experimental work comprises two studies, both by Baltes and Zerbe, published in 1976.

Research Question 2: What environmental conditions in the naturally existing ecology of the elderly foster and maintain dependent behaviors? How does the staff member or family member react when the elderly person does ask for help, or when she does not button her shirt, or when she does attempt to write a letter or read a book or take a bath? We need to observe systematically what happens when an elderly person exhibits dependent or independent behaviors. Our sequential observational studies with institutionalized elderly comprise five studies: the first three were conducted while I was at the Pennsylvania State University (Baltes, Burgess, & Stewart, 1980; Baltes, Honn, Barton, Orzech, & Lago, 1983; Barton, Baltes, & Orzech, 1980); these were followed by two studies conducted during my affiliation with the Free University in Berlin, Germany (Baltes, Kindermann, & Reisenzein, 1986; Baltes, Kindermann, Reisenzein, & Schmid, 1987).

As you will see later, the observational findings have prompted three subquestions:

Research Question 2a: Are the observed interaction patterns between elderly and their social partners generalizable from the institutional settings to community settings? To address this question we conducted a sequential observational study with elderly living in the community (Baltes & Wahl, 1992; Wahl & Baltes, 1990).

Research Question 2b: Are the interaction patterns age-specific? To answer this question we conducted comparative work with both institutionalized and noninstitutionalized children (Baltes, Reisenzein, & Kindermann, 1985; Kindermann, 1993).

Research Question 3: What are possible reasons for the dominance of the dependency-support pattern? Or specifically, what explains the behavior of social partners? To this effect we designed and executed three studies using interview and experimental data. Wahl (1991) asked staff and residents immediately after the observations why they did what they did, trying to get at attributions of dependency and independence by staff and residents. Reichert (1993) attempted to manipulate expectations of competence and incompetence toward elderly held by social partners and analyzed their effect on behaviors. Finally, Schmid-Furstoss (1990) asked elderly people living in institutions and in the community about their understanding of the concepts independence and dependence.

Research Question 4: Can we change these interaction patterns? For instance, can we teach social partners such as staff, spouses, or grandchildren to pay more attention to independent behaviors of the elderly, to assess their strengths, and to avoid providing assistance where it is not needed or not even wanted? Can we change the environment such that we avoid overcare, overprotection, and paternalism toward the elderly? For this purpose we developed a training program for staff and tested its effect in a study conducted by Baltes, Neumann, and Zank (1994).

The most recent question with which I am struggling has to do with considerations concerning the justification of intervention in the context of dependency. These considerations are not foremost fed by ethical concerns. It is instead an empirical research question over whether or not behavioral dependency requires change under any circumstances. At the end of the book I try to address this question and come to the conclusion that some dependencies might be self-selected and part of successful aging, and thus should not be intervened upon.

Experimental Field Studies: Behavioral Plasticity

RESEARCH QUESTION 1: *Are Dependent Behaviors of the Elderly Modifiable?*

STUDIES 1 AND 2 (Baltes & Zerbe, 1976a,b)

As to the modifiability of dependent behavior, operant-experimental work, including our studies as well as those by other researchers, has revealed substantial behavioral plasticity in the elderly (for reviews see Baltes 1982, 1988; Baltes & Barton, 1977, 1979; Hoyer, 1974; Hussian, 1981; Mosher-Ashley, 1986–1987; Patterson & Jackson, 1980, 1981; Wisocki, 1984). Findings strongly support the modifiability of older people's behavior, even its reversibility as in the case of dependent behaviors.

Changes resulted either from changing discriminative stimuli or from changing reinforcing stimuli. Changing discriminative stimuli might mean the elderly person use eating utensils with thickened handles for having better grip or wear clothing with few buttons or zippers to make dressing easier, or using cues or prompts to initiate or maintain a behavior. The use of reinforcement might mean taking a walk after having dressed oneself, or listening to music after having eaten independently. These studies demonstrated the possibility of health intervention in long-term care facilities other than by means of physical or medical care. They also demonstrated that elderly people could relearn proper self-care behaviors subsequent to environmental changes, which would again reinforce independent behaviors. The important role of both social and physical environmental factors in influencing the level of functioning of the elderly is underlined. Reversibility of dependent behaviors strengthens the notion that environmental conditions codetermine the acquisition and maintenance of dependency in institutionalized elderly (see Baltes & Zerbe, 1976a,b).

Although the different studies had different foci, there were some essential common elements in design and approach: Subjects were mostly long-term nursing home residents who had no direct physical impairments that would prohibit the relearning of the desired behavior; target dependent behaviors had existed for a long time; a single-subject design was chosen; and change procedures consisted of reinforcement contingencies sometimes coupled with stimulus control procedures.

One illustration from our work will suffice here to make the point. In this study (see also Baltes & Zerbe, 1976a) the target dependent behavior to be changed was "not eating by himself." The subject was a 79-year-old man whose overall dependency was initiated, in large part, by a stroke he had suffered some time ago but was thereafter maintained by environmental conditions in the nursing home. He could move arms and hands quite well. Stimulus control and reinforcement procedures were utilized to re-establish self-feeding behavior. The stimulus control procedure consisted of providing the man with eating utensils that he could grasp and handle more easily, thus compensating for his somewhat stiff and crippled fingers. As reinforcement following any instance of self-feeding (i.e., bringing food to his mouth and eating it), continuous and immediate social praise was delivered by the man's wife, by other table companions, as well as by the experimenter. Figure 2 shows the experimental design used and the findings.

It can readily be seen that during baseline observations self-feeding occurred at a very low rate, whereas an increase in self-

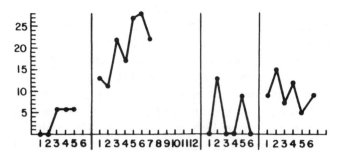

Figure 2. Findings of a behavior modification study using an ABAB de-sign (baseline, intervention, baseline, intervention) to change the fre-quency in self-feeding.

feeding was observed after the introduction of the treatment phase. A decrease occurred, as expected, when the situation re-verted to baseline conditions. Reintroduction of the treatment phase led again to an increase in self-feeding behavior, although the effect failed to stabilize. When the situation was examined, it became rather obvious that a change in the reinforcement pro-cedure not under the control of the experimenter had taken place: The wife was absent from the table because she had fallen ill. Discussions with the old man revealed that he not only missed his wife and her reinforcers but that he also was worried about her sickness and afraid she might die. He indirectly asked for the treatment to be discontinued.

I have chosen this study for inclusion because we can see that environmental events, both the experimental manipulation (treat-ment phases) and the "uncontrolled" manipulation by the ex-traexperimental ecology (his wife's absence), demonstrate the impact environmental factors can have on behavior.

This study and a number of other experiments (for reviews see Baltes & Barton, 1977, 1979; Mosher-Ashley, 1986–1987) have shown that aging behaviors, such as dependent behaviors, can be changed through both therapeutic (reinforcement) and prosthetic (stimulus control) environmental events. This conclusion concern-ing modifiability or plasticity of behavior of the elderly is sup-ported by most other experimental studies dealing not only with dependent behaviors, but also with a gamut of others (for instance, with cognitive behaviors see Baltes & Lindenberger, 1988). The only time behavioral treatment is questionable is when the problem behavior is associated with direct biological or physical incapacitation. Even in those instances, however, compensation or rehabilitation through prosthetic devices can be achieved.

Such evidence for plasticity or modifiability of dependent behaviors of elderly people was rather novel in the mid-1970s (for review see Baltes & Barton, 1979). Since then it has become one small mosaic in the well-established notion of sizable plasticity in aging (P. B. Baltes, 1987). The important conclusion from this early experimental work is that it is not always lack of competence due to physical or mental impairment that is at the root of behavioral dependency, but rather that environmental factors are at least co-responsible for its development and maintenance.

Such early operant-experimental work would rarely be classified as "true" intervention, since most effects vanished shortly after the experimenter left the setting. The reasons for this are manifold. Most commonly, the discriminative stimuli and reinforcing consequences used in treatment procedures were not inherent in the setting. Thus, the end of the experiment or the departure of the experimenter often reintroduced baseline conditions (in contrast, see an attempt to change staff behavior by Sperbeck & Whitbourne, 1981, or our own intervention work to be reported under Question 4).

For our discussion it is of great importance to emphasize that the evidence of modifiability of even long-standing dependent behaviors negates the assumption that dependency is primarily the consequence of lack or loss of competence in the elderly. On the contrary, the elderly in many cases still display competencies and still possess the basic skills to perform the task at hand when given the opportunity or when they are prompted or reinforced. The findings from operant-experimental work support the possibility of behavioral optimization and corrective compensation in old age and the importance of both physical and social environmental factors for functioning well of the elderly. Environmental conditions are among the more important (although perhaps not necessary) conditions involved in the acquisition, maintenance, and modification of dependent behavior. Reversibility of dependent behaviors justifies a systematic search for conditions in the natural environment at large that foster dependency in the elderly.

Now the question facing us is to find out what environmental conditions in the naturally existing life conditions of the elderly foster and maintain dependent behaviors.

5

Observational Research in Institutional Settings

Now that we have established that the dependent behaviors of the type we are interested in are reversible or at least modifiable, we have to ask ourselves what in the natural environment fosters these dependent behaviors.

RESEARCH QUESTION 2: *What Environmental Conditions Foster and Maintain Dependent Behaviors in the Elderly?*

Sequential Observational Studies: The Dependency–Support Script and Independence–Ignore Script

The main aspect of the observational studies is an account of environmental conditions involved in the maintenance of dependent behaviors. Direct observation of the behavior of the elderly and their partners in the natural environment of institutional or community settings is used to identify and analyze naturally existing social environmental consequences of dependency.

How did we collect the data? To answer this question let me give a complete rundown about the technical side of the observations. In order to get reliable and valid data we needed to develop a behavior-coding scheme, train observers, design and standardize the observational procedure.

Development of the Behavior-Coding System: A Behavior-Mapping Study. The behavior categories of the observational coding system were based on the findings of a behavior-mapping study (Baltes, Barton, Orzech, & Lago, 1983). *Behavior mapping* is a technique used in environmental psychology that has its roots in the familiar architect's floor plan (Ittelson, Rivlin, & Proshansky, 1970). The technique of behavior mapping allows for the collection of all behaviors exhibited by the elderly resident and the staff, thus providing a complete behavioral repertoire for both in the institutional setting.

Design and Procedure. Using a floor plan of the nursing home, two observers recorded all behaviors of all elderly residents (N = 113; 77 received intermediate care, 36 skilled nursing care), aged 60 through 97 (mean age 70) with time of institutionalization ranging from a few weeks to 5 years, from 7 a.m. to 7 p.m. During that time all staff members ($N = 12$) responsible for the residents during the two day shifts were observed as well. For two days two observers made a total of 48 prescribed round trips through the nursing home (see Figure 3) and registered type of behavior, location, and position separately for residents and staff. In all, they recorded 960 minutes of observation time and registered 2,141 behavioral events for residents and 540 for staff (see Figures 4 and 5).

These concrete behaviors were then grouped in categories and labeled as dependent self-care, independent self-care, or behaviors that were nonengaged, constructively engaged, destructively engaged, dependence-supportive, independence-supportive, and so forth. Table 1 shows a summary of all observed behaviors and their classification in behavior categories. In this sense, the behavior categories for both the target elderly and their social partners focused exclusively on overt and concrete acts related to everyday independence and dependency in the context of self-care and of activities best described as leisure activities.

The Basic Behavior-Coding Scheme. With regard to independence-related behaviors, we differentiated between self-care and engaged – prosocial or constructively engaged and asocial or destructively engaged – behaviors (see Table 2). The independent self-care category includes such behaviors as getting dressed, eating, and toileting. Constructively engaged behaviors include behaviors such as reading, writing, playing games, and watching television. Destructively engaged behaviors include such behaviors as quarrelling, hitting, throwing food, and screaming. With regard to dependency-related behaviors, we differentiated between

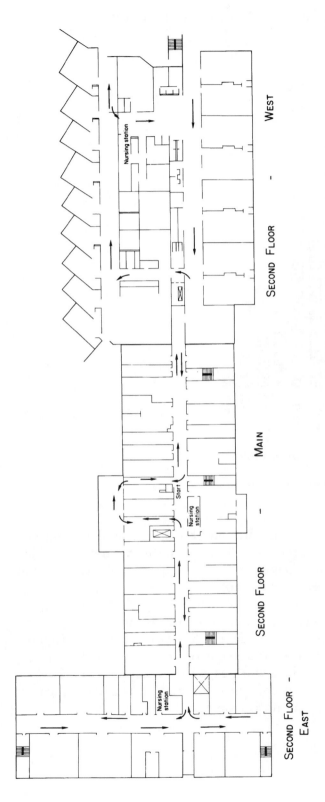

Figure 3. Floor plan of the behavior mapping study.

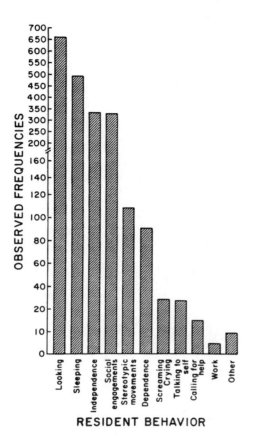

Figure 4. Behaviors of residents.

dependent self-care (being dressed or fed, etc.) and nonengaged behaviors (staring at the wall). Sleeping during the day was added later as a separate category, since we did not want to overload the nonengaged behavior category.

Behavior of staff was coded in five categories, too: independence-supportive behaviors (any encouragement of independent or discouragement of dependent behavior), dependence-supportive behaviors (any encouragement of dependent or discouragement of independent behavior), engagement-supportive behaviors (any encouragement of constructively and obstructively engaged behavior), leaving, and no response.

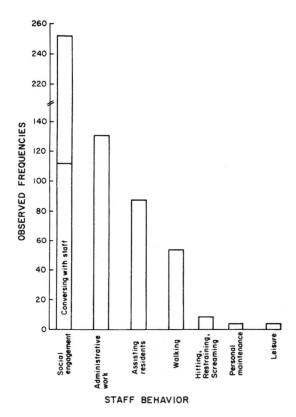

Figure 5. Behaviors of staff.

The following are some examples of possible behavior sequences and their codings.

Antecedent event: dependent behavior (05) of resident, *who is sitting in front of the food tray staring at it.*
Possible consequences:

a. *"Good for you that you are waiting for me to feed you"*; this response would be coded 09, a dependence-supportive behavior. It would be considered a behavior complementary or congruent to 05.
b. *"Come on, you can eat by yourself"*; this would be coded 08, an independence-supportive, noncomplementary or incongruent behavior by staff.

Table 1. *Classification of All Behaviors Observed for Residents and Staff*

Independent Personal Maintenance Behavior of Resident
Resident's bathing, dressing, eating, grooming, toileting, ambulating without assistance, or resident's statements of intent to accomplish these tasks unaided. Anything the resident does to accomplish these tasks is considered independent, even if the act consists only of an initiation. Examples: Resident holds own toothbrush; complies with staff member's instruction to pick up foot so shoe can be put on; wheels self unaided; sits alone on toilet; buttons own shirt.

Dependent Personal Maintenance Behavior of Resident
Resident's request for or acceptance of assistance in bathing, dressing, eating, grooming, toileting, or ambulating. Can also refer to resident's refusal to perform such tasks or components thereof. Examples: Resident calls for help; does not lift foot when asked; walks only with support from staff; is pushed in a wheelchair; does not comply with staff requests or instructions to get out of bed.

Constructively Engaged Behavior of Resident
Resident's behavior that is unrelated to personal maintenance but is socially appropriate, e.g., letter writing, conversing, watching TV, reading, playing games, knitting, helping others.

Nonengagement-Supportive Behavior of Social Partner
Verbal or physical behaviors of staff, visitors, volunteers, or other residents that encourage or elicit nonengagement or cessation of a resident behavior. Examples: ties resident to chair; instructs resident to sit still and be quiet; praises resident for taking a nap; expresses disapproval of an activity; wants not to be bothered.

Independence-Supportive Behavior of Social Partner
Behaviors of staff, visitors, volunteers, or fellow residents that encourage (praise) or elicit (instruct, suggest) resident bathing, dressing, grooming, eating, toileting and ambulating. Examples: "Put on your sweater." "You can walk by yourself." "That's a good job you did shaving this morning." "I am glad you ate your breakfast all by yourself." "Time to get up." Visitor hugs resident who walks unaided to greet him.

Dependence-Supportive Behavior of Social Partner
Verbal or physical behaviors of staff, visitors, volunteers, or fellow residents that encourage (praise) or elicit (instruct, suggest) resident's request for or acceptance of assistance in bathing, dressing, eating, grooming, toileting, or ambulating. Examples: "Let me help you with that." "I'll ask the aide to do that." "Mother, you sit down." Caresses resident while she cries for help. Roommate wheels resident to dining room.

Table 1. (*cont.*)

No Response of Social Partner
Occasions when staff, visitors, volunteers, or fellow residents are in
the vicinity (within 6 feet) of the resident, but do not direct any verbal
or physical behavior toward him.

Leaving of Social Partner
Occasions when staff, visitor, volunteer, or fellow resident who was
previously within 6 feet of resident leaves the area.

Antecedent event: dependent behavior (05) of resident, who says, *"I
cannot wash my face."*
Possible consequences:

a. *Staff member takes the washcloth and washes the resident's face.*
   This would be coded 09, a dependence-supportive complementary
   behavior;
b. *Staff member explains how she should wash her face;* this would be
   considered a noncomplementary response (08) that is, independence-
   supportive behavior;
c. *Resident goes on washing his or her face;* this would be an independent behavior of the resident himself or herself (04) as a consequent
   event.

Antecedent event: independent behavior (04) of residents. *Resident is
putting on his shirt* (04).
Possible consequences:

a. *Staff member takes shirt away from resident and starts dressing the
   resident;* this is a noncomplementary response, namely 09, dependence-supportive behavior;
b. *Staff member is watching and smiling at the resident;* this is coded
   as a complementary response, 08, independence-supportive behavior;
c. *Resident puts on shoes;* this is a continuation of resident independent behavior, 04;
d. *"I told you not to dress yourself, you always get it wrong";* this is a noncomplementary behavior of staff, 09, dependence-supportive behavior.

Variations in the Basic Coding Scheme. In the course of our
research few changes were made to the basic coding scheme that
allows for coding of the person who is behaving (elderly focus vs.
social partner), for the presence of other people (solitary vs. social), and for the type of behavior. At different times we added

Table 2. *Coding Scheme for Behaviors Observed*

Input	Code	Category Name
Actor	03	Visitor
	04	Volunteer
	05	Group of social partners
Type of behavior		
Target person	00	Sleeping
	01	Constructively engaged behavior
	02	Destructively engaged behavior
	03	Nonengaged behavior
	04	Independent self-care behavior
	05	Dependent self-care behavior
Social partner	06	Engagement-supportive behavior
	07	Nonengagement-supportive behavior
	08	Independence-supportive behavior
	09	Dependence-supportive behavior
	11	Leaving
Dyadic form of behavior	1	Suggestion/command/request
	2	Intention
	3	Compliance/cooperation
	4	Refusal/resistance
	5	Conversation
	6	Miscellaneous other
Flow of behavior	1	Change in behavior category
	2	Same behavior in same category
	3	New behavior in same category

codes to specify the dyadic form, in which the behavior was exhibited, codes to specify the continuation or discontinuation of behaviors, or codes to identify the type of context (eating, washing, dressing, etc.; see Table 2).

The reason for adding the category *dyadic form* was our interest in specifying more clearly the directionality of the interaction; that is, who is attempting to change or control whom? We were interested in only five forms, namely suggestion/request/command, intention, compliance/cooperation, refusal/resistance, and conversation. All of the behaviors that did not fit into any one of these five form categories were coded as miscellaneous other.

The *suggestion/request/command* category was coded when the observed behavior represented an act that asked the interacting partner to pay attention and to do something. Examples include: "Would you lift my foot?" and "Get out of bed!"

The *intention* category was coded when the observed behavior represented an act directed at future behavior to be carried out by the actor him- or herself. Examples include: "I will go to the barber today," "I will have nurse Olga give me a bath today," or "I am going to eat now."

The *compliance/cooperation* category was coded when the observed behavior represented the willingness to do something that had been asked for directly by a social partner or indirectly by some existing rules in the institution. Examples include the following: Resident allows himself to be dressed after being told to do so by a staff member; two residents play a game together; a staff member gets the medicine a resident has asked for.

The *refusal/resistance* category was coded when the observed behavior expressed disobedience or rejection of a demand made by a social partner. Examples include: Resident turns his back when asked to participate in a game; staff person says: "You cannot have your medicine now, I am too busy"; resident starts dressing herself after having been asked by staff to wait until she has come back.

The category of *conversation* was reserved for behaviors representing verbal interactions, such as talking about the weather, family members, or food.

The category *miscellaneous other* was used when a behavior did not fit any of the other categories. Note that all behaviors of the residents in the absence of social partners had to be coded as *other,* except behaviors expressed in the form of intention.

This category system of dyadic form was used in the studies by Baltes et al. (1987) and Baltes and Wahl (1992).

Continuity and discontinuity of behavioral events became of major interest, in relation to the question whether independent and dependent behaviors were perhaps of genuinely different duration. Therefore, in the case of a behavior with a duration of more than 10 seconds reinforcing reactions by staff, for instance, would not come after the first coding, but perhaps after the second or tenth. To allow for differentiation between continuous and discontinuous behavioral events within the response class of independent behaviors, each resident behavior was identified as either old or ongoing, or new. The latter signified a change in behavior within the same response class. A change across response classes, i.e., independent to dependent, etc. automatically was coded as new (see Study 7).

Apparatus for Collecting Sequential Observations. Since we were interested in interaction patterns we needed to observe and code the behavioral stream. For this reason, trained observers coded the naturally occurring behavior sequences during daily routines. Portable, battery-powered event recorders (Datamyte and Datapad) were used for data collection, storage (in the exact sequence of input), and computer interface functions. Observers were trained to record naturally occurring behavior sequences using the behavior-coding system and the electronic recorder.

Observer Training and Reliability. Observations were collected by observers trained by the author or her senior collaborators. Because the research program was conducted over a lengthy period of time, from 1977 until 1990, and in different locations, first in Pennsylvania in the United States, then in Berlin, Germany, different observers were involved in different settings. The training was, however, supervised by the same trainer (the author) with the same training manual that had been used in all the studies.

The training program consists of seven steps: (1) memorizing all codes by heart; (2) paper-and-pencil coding of transcripts of real interactions; (3) paper-and-pencil coding of videotaped interactions; (4) familiarization with apparatus (Datamyte or Datapad) using transcribed material; (5) coding with apparatus from video material; (6) paper-and-pencil coding of live interactions in the field; and finally, (7) coding interactions in situ in the field with the help of the apparatus. Progress from step to step depends on the level of interrater reliability.

In the institutional setting, in general, two observers were scheduled randomly for each observational period, each one observing half the focus residents. This setup allowed the two observers to observe simultaneously two randomly selected residents either at the beginning or the end of each observation period. Based on the simultaneously collected data, reliabilities were computed separately for each day of observation. We used the kappa statistics because it provides a chance-corrected coefficient of agreement, in contrast to a percentage correct agreement. Perfect agreement ($\kappa = 1$) implied a point-by-point correspondence of the two observers' sequential protocols. Kappas ranged above .70, which can be considered satisfactory.

Observational Procedure, Observational Session, Observational Unit, and Total Observation Time. Periods of observation were selected for their high level of interactions occurring at these times. In the institutional setting, the morning (from 6 a.m. to 9 a.m.), midday (from 11 a.m. to 1 p.m.), and evening (from 5 p.m. to 7 p.m.) were high interaction times and therefore chosen for observation sessions. Save for the first two studies (Baltes, Burgess, & Stewart, 1980; Barton, Baltes, & Orzech, 1980), all subsequent studies with older persons in long-term care institutions used all three observation sessions. Each session lasted about 2 hours, with each focus person being observed for 3 minutes each session for between 15 and 20 days.

Observations of the behavioral sequences between focus person and partner began when the observer encountered the focus person (allowing for a short warm-up period, usually an exchange of greetings). The behavioral stream was coded in 10-second observational units continuously for the duration of the entire session. A behavior of the focus person was always recorded first, and thereafter behaviors were recorded in turns, unless the partner left the room or the behavior of the focus person continued longer than 10 seconds and the partner did not respond within the 10-second interval. The score–rescore criterion of 10 seconds had been selected empirically. It was long enough to reflect the natural reaction pattern on the part of staff and short enough to avoid too many re-recordings of ongoing behaviors of residents. The existence of the score–rescore criterion was critical for statistical analyses in that it provided a standardization of the duration of behaviors of focus persons and partners. In the case of simultaneous behaviors exhibited by the focus person or the staff, the rule was to code self-care behaviors first and any other concurrent behavior (like conversation about the weather) second.

Study Design. Most of the observational studies were short-term studies lasting two to three weeks with daily observations of each target resident. In two studies (Baltes et al., 1983, 1987), however, we followed the residents over a 6-month period, with the aim of picking up any changes that might occur in newly admitted residents.

Data Analysis. Data collection of this kind yields huge data sets; in our case we often had to deal with more than 20,000 behavioral events. To handle and understand the data, we used simple reductive methods, such as probability matrixes of contingencies. Observational data collected with detailed temporal relationships between events can be analyzed on at least two levels: the frequency level and the sequential pattern level.

Behavior Profile: Frequency Analyses. To gain an understanding of the behavioral profiles of the elderly and their social partners, we usually used analyses of variance techniques or log linear analyses.

Interaction Patterns: Sequential Lag Analyses. Sequential patterns are deduced from recurrent orderings of events across the behavioral chains of the interactants. The presence of interchain connections or interchain causality can be inferred. The latter, however, needs additional testing with the help of intervention research (see under Research Question 4). Interchain connections are inferred when knowledge of one actor's behavior reduces uncertainty about the subsequent behavior of the other actor (Gottman, 1979).

The computer program LAGS (Sackett, Holm, Crowley, & Henkins, 1979) is an analytic strategy to detect recurrent sequences in the stream of interactions. A differentiation is made between baseline probability, that is the probability that an event A – say a dependence-supportive behavior – will occur anywhere in the behavioral sequence, and conditional probability, that is the probability that event A will follow a specified event B, for instance dependent behavior (Lag 1). Unconditional or baseline probabilities are estimated as the frequency of event A compared to the sum of all other behavioral events. Conditional probabilities are deviations from these baseline expectations (Lag 0). If deviations are shown to be significant (binomial z test), one speaks of a certain degree of "temporal" predictability or control of A over B (control index). The analysis is sequential because it deals with the temporal order of resident- and partner-related events. It is conditional because it specifies the preceding events and the "if" condition for which the probability of differing subsequent events is examined; for example, if a dependent behavior of the elderly occurred dependence-supportive behavior of staff will most likely happen next.

The target events in these studies are all elderly residents' behaviors, since the goal of our study is to ascertain the social contingencies succeeding their occurrence. For these target events, statistically significant deviations of the conditional probability from the base probability of a consequent event are identified. The conditional probabilities are computed for behavioral events, one (Lag 1), two (Lag 2), three (Lag 3), . . . units (lags) removed from the criterion behaviors. Such computation of lags provides a representation of the time-extended order of events following the criterion behavior (for a more detailed description of the statistical procedure see Barton et al., 1980). The statistical program LAGS (Allison & Liker, 1982; Sackett et al., 1979) served as the data-analytical framework.

Patterson (1982) refers to the statistical existence of contingencies using the term "control." He suggests computing power indexes in addition to control indexes in order to explain the variance of the contingency accounted for by the antecedent event. The power indexes tell us, in the presence of statistically significant control, the percentage of behavior B that occur if behavior A was the temporal precursor. In principle, one can have significant conditional probabilities (linking behavior B to behavior A), that is, significant control indexes but high or low power of A over B. For example, in the case of a conditional probability of .20 (i.e., in 20% of the time B follows A), all Bs could be accounted for by this temporal relationship. This would present a case of perfect power of A over B, even though B occurs only 20% of the time but all 20% following A. In contrast, the same .20 conditional probability linking B to A could evince low power, such as .10. This would mean that even though 20% of the time B follows A, there are many Bs, that is 90%, that are not preceded by A.

Sequential lag analysis not only helps determine which environmental event (in this case the behavior of social partner) follows a behavior of the old person, but also helps us look at the other side of the coin to see which behaviors of the old person follow which behaviors of the social partner. We can then study the direction of behavioral influences as well as the reciprocity of influences between residents and social partners.

In order to illustrate the findings and paint a comprehensive picture of them, let me describe the specific research questions and results of the studies in the sequence they had been planned and executed. This will show quite clearly that each study was built on the preceding one and was intended to answer one or more additional questions. Two related studies will not be described here, the study by Lester and Baltes (1978), a pilot study, and the dissertation study by Barton (1978) using simple rather than sequential observations.

Institutional Settings. The selection of institutional environments was guided, aside from practical reasons, by the notion that such environments represent extreme conditions of the social ecology of aging in general. In this vein, we consider them as simulations (P. B. Baltes & Goulet, 1971) or research analogues of the socialization situation in old age. We have already mentioned that nursing homes come to enjoy a degree of control and power over their clients that normally only parents are allowed over their children. Despite the legal status of most nursing home residents as free citizens, they share much with children, psychiatric patients, and even prisoners. Control over many aspects of life in long-term care institutions for the elderly is common. In addition, the elderly entering an institution are often experiencing certain losses and are looking for a less demanding environment. Thus, institutions seem to be the most likely place to encounter dependency. *Five studies* will be reported here (Baltes, Burgess, & Stewart, 1980; Baltes, Honn, Barton, Orzech, & Lago, 1983; Baltes, Kindermann, & Reisenzein, 1986; Baltes, Kindermann, Reisenzein, & Schmid, 1987; Barton, Baltes, & Orzech, 1980), all of which are based on observations of the behavioral and social world of the elderly in institutions.

Data were collected in long-term care institutions in the United States (Pennsylvania) and Germany (Berlin). These included proprietary and nonproprietary homes; homes that were religiously affiliated, state-owned and private; homes that were old and modern; homes that seemed comfortable and personal and homes that seemed sterile and anonymous. In the majority of these homes there were two beds per room; a few had one or three beds per room. In the home for the chronically ill there were mostly four beds per room. The major difference between American and German homes was that in Germany doors to the rooms of residents are kept closed. This closed-door policy obviously made our observations more obtrusive in the German homes than in the American homes.

Samples. Residents who were the focus of our studies were recruited randomly from the resident population in each home. The target populations comprised persons over 65 who were not completely bedbound, severely confused, nor acutely ill. They all were oriented to person and place, but many of them asked the observer every day what she or he were doing in the home. They all received either intermediate or skilled nursing care. The samples are, thus, representative of a large portion of the elderly population in long-term care institutions.

Elderly residents were approached individually for informed consent or, depending on the home's policy, only the administrator's consent was needed. A total of about 230 institutionalized elderly (summed across all studies) have been observed. Each study comprised about 40 residents. The residents were mostly women (with roughly a ratio of 7 to 1), who came from the middle to lower-middle social classes. They varied as to their medical problems, their years of institutionalization, and age. Medical problems reported most frequently in their records were arteriosclerosis, cardiovascular diseases, and cerebral arteriosclerosis. In terms of care, more participants received intermediate than skilled nursing care in all homes except in the home for the chronically ill. Here there were more participants receiving skilled care. Age varied from 65 to 97. In most homes the average age was between 80 and 84. Years of institutionalization ranged from 2 months to more than 84 months. The average length of time in the different homes amounted to about 2.9 years, except in the home for the chronically ill, which had an average of 4 years of institutionalization.

As to the social ecology, we were mostly interested in the staff and the staff's behavior. To get a more complete picture of the social ecology, however, in some studies we observed fellow residents, visitors, volunteers, and other health professionals. Most of these potential social agents, after being asked to participate, volunteered. There were very few refusals. (Overall, there were more refusals in German nursing homes than in American nursing homes.)

STUDY 3 (Baltes, Burgess, & Stewart, 1980)

The question addressed in this first sequential observational study was: What is the natural context of dependent and independent behaviors of the elderly during self-care situations?

Approximately 44 hours of observations of behavior sequences during mornings were obtained over 11 days ($N = 48$ residents and $N = 6$ staff members). A total of 1,948 observations were recorded. Table 3 shows, for the three target behaviors of residents (independent, dependent, and other behavior), the proportions and raw frequencies of each staff behavior observed in interaction with the target residents. Figure 6 illustrates the results.

The main effects of the analysis of variance indicate that, during self-care situations, residents more frequently engage in independent behavior than in any other. The interaction effects between resident and staff behaviors show supportive staff behavior (reinforcement) following dependent behaviors and no response following independent behaviors. One can interpret these findings as suggesting a fairly consistent and immediate positive reinforcement schedule for dependent behaviors of the elderly resident and an extinction schedule for independent behaviors. A discussion of these findings will follow the next study (Study 4) since we will see the same results.

Table 3. Resident–Staff Sequences for Each Staff Member Summed across All Observations and Residents

Resident Behaviors	Staff Independence-Supporting Behaviors							Staff Dependence-Supporting Behaviors							Staff, Other Behaviors							Staff, No Response						
	1	2	3	4	5	6	12	1	2	3	4	5	6	12	1	2	3	4	5	6	12	1	2	3	4	5	6	12
Independent Behavior	.04[a]	.08	.11	.19	.24	.04	.13	.1	.21	.21	.19	.34	.18	.37	.00	.03	.03	.09	.08	.00	.00	.84	.68	.64	.59	.34	.78	.50
	6[b]	22	27	47	64	4	9	17	59	50	49	92	18	25	0	8	8	8	24	0	0	125	187	153	148	92	78	34
Dependent Behavior	.03	.06	.02	.13	.13	.00	.00	.74	.78	.85	.56	.79	1.0	1.0	.06	.02	.06	.00	.00	.00	.00	.16	.14	.06	.31	.08	.00	.00
	1	3	1	4	3	0	0	23	40	40	18	19	6	19	2	1	3	0	0	0	0	5	7	3	10	2	0	0
Other Behavior	.00	.02	.05	.10	.13	.00	.00	.22	.15	.31	.33	.29	.29	.20	.30	.21	.36	.17	.37	.14	.45	.48	.62	.28	.40	.21	.51	.35
	0	2	5	9	19	0	0	5	14	33	30	40	2	4	7	19	38	16	56	1	9	11	57	30	37	32	4	7

[a]First value represents mean proportions of behaviors per staff members within each behavior category across all observations and residents.

[b]Second value represents mean behavioral frequencies across all observations and residents per staff member.
Column head numbers 1 to 6 and 12 indicate the 7 staff members.

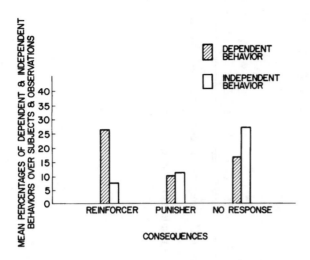

Figure 6. Behavior frequencies of staff behaviors, classified as reinforcer, punisher, or no response following two behaviors, dependent and independent, of residents.

STUDY 4 (Barton, Baltes, & Orzech, 1980)

This study was a replication of the previous study, although conducted in a different nursing home. At the same time it was our first attempt to use Sackett's lag sequential analysis.

In this study, we again only observed in the mornings, the self-care situations, and worked with five behavior categories (independent and dependent behaviors of elderly, independence- and dependence-supportive behaviors of staff, and a category of other behavior).

The findings are summarized first for the behavior profiles of residents and staff and then for the interaction analyses. The frequencies and base probabilities for each behavior are shown in Figure 7 separately for residents and staff. A total of 2,030 observations of residents and staff were recorded. Of those, 1,428 observations referred to behaviors that occurred in the presence of staff. For resident behavior, note first that the most frequently observed behavior was independent behavior, with a frequency of 246 events. Dependent behavior was recorded 174 times. This frequency profile represents a 1.4:1 ratio for independent to dependent behavior. As to staff behavior, the most frequent be-

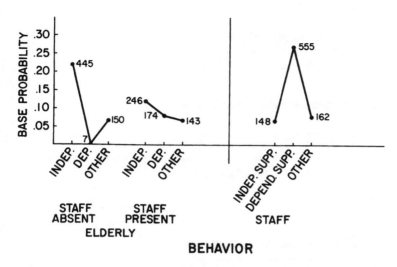

Figure 7. Behavior frequencies and base probabilities for each behavior of residents and staff.

havior was dependence-supportive behavior, with an overall frequency of 555 acts. Independence-supportive behavior by staff involved only 148 acts. This outcome can be described as a 3.7: 1 ratio of dependence-supportive to independence-supportive behavior of staff. Dependence-or independence-related behavior of staff and residents involved close to 79% of the observations.

The interaction patterns are illustrated in Figures 8 and 9 for four behaviors following the two criterion behaviors, namely independent and dependent behavior of residents. The figures include a horizontal band indexing the confidence range of the expected base probability for the respective consequent event. Let us first look at independent behavior and its consequences shown in Figure 8 and Table 4. Here you find the salient information about four consequent events following the criterion independent behavior of residents: independence-supportive and dependence-supportive behaviors of staff as well as two types of behavior of the focus resident, namely dependent and independent behavior.

As you can see, at Lag 1 the four consequent events account for 80% of all events following the criterion behavior. Independent behavior had a base probability of .12. The most frequent

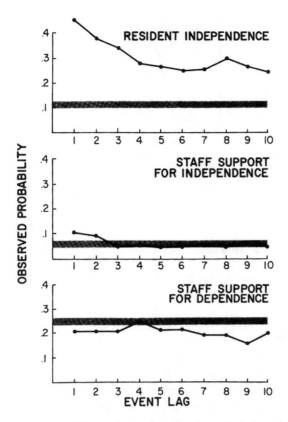

Figure 8. Base and conditional probability at 10 lags for three consequent behaviors following an instance of independent behaviors of residents.

consequent event was a continuation of the resident's independent
behavior. From Lag 1 through Lag 10, conditional probabilities
for resident independent behavior ranged from .44 at Lag 1 to
.25 at Lag 10. Thus, on the average, in Lags 1 to 10 independent
behavior significantly exceeded its base probability. Thus, if a resident exhibited an instance of independent behavior it was likely
that he would continue exhibiting more independent acts.

The next likely consequent event was dependence-supportive
behavior by staff, although at a rate lower than its base probability of .26. At all lags but Lag 4, dependence-supportive behaviors follow independent behavior with a conditional probability

Table 4. *Conditional Probabilities for Each Resident and Staff Behavior Given Residents' Independent Behavior as Criterion Event*

Behavior	Event Lag										Confidence Interval
	1	2	3	4	5	6	7	8	9	10	
Independent behavior	.44**	.38**	.34**	.28**	.27**	.25**	.26**	.30**	.27**	.25**	.13–.10
Dependent behavior	.04*	.07	.09	.07	.10	.08	.09	.07	.08	.07	.10–.07
Independence-supportive behavior	.11**	.09**	.05	.06	.05	.05	.06	.05	.07	.05	.07–.05
Dependence-supportive behavior	.21*	.21*	.21*	.25	.22*	.22*	.19*	.19*	.16*	.20*	.28–.24

*Significantly less than base probability ($p < .05$).
**Significantly more than base probability ($p < .05$).

ranging from .21 to .16. We interpret the deviations at Lag 4 as a chance outcome.

Independence-supportive behavior by staff was influenced by the criterion behavior. However, its conditional probability was affected less than the first two consequent behaviors together. Specifically, it rose significantly above its base probability of .06 to .11 at Lag 1 and to .09 at Lag 2.

Dependent behavior by the resident as the fourth possible consequent event was not affected by the criterion behavior.

Let us now look at the consequent events following dependent behavior of residents. Table 5 and Figure 9 summarize this information. Again, four subsequent events were considered. These represented 98% of all events recorded at Lag 1.

Dependent behavior by residents in the presence of staff had a base probability of .08 (Figure 9). Note again that this base rate was lower than that for independent behavior by residents. The behavior flow following dependent behaviors shows dependence-supportive behavior by staff to be the most frequent consequent event. This is particularly obvious for Lag 1, when its conditional probability was .58 compared to its base rate of .26. There continued to be a statistically significant elevation in staff support for dependence for the remaining lags ranging in conditional probability between .30 and .37.

The second most likely consequent event was more dependent behavior by the resident. Except for Lag 1, there was a statistically significant elevation for all lags ranging from .31 to .13.

Independence-supportive behavior by staff was also affected by the antecedent event, dependent behavior. As was true for the examination of resident independence as a criterion, however, the effect (departure from the base-rate probability) was not dramatic. First, staff support for independence was relatively low in probability to begin with, exhibiting a base probability of .06. When observed as a consequence to resident dependent behavior, this probability was elevated only slightly (though with statistical significance) for most lags, ranging from base rate to .12. Staff appeared to show only little differential behavior (dependence- vs. independence-supportive) as a function of resident behavior.

Independent behavior by residents was not affected in its base probability by the antecedent event, dependent behavior. Indepen-

Table 5. *Conditional Probabilities for Each Resident and Staff Behavior Given Residents' Dependent Behavior as Criterion Event*

Behavior	Event Lag										Confidence Interval
	1	2	3	4	5	6	7	8	9	10	
Dependent behavior	.07	.31**	.16**	.27**	.19**	.16**	.22**	.16**	.16**	.13**	.10–.07
Independent behavior	.10	.12	.14**	.13	.10	.15**	.11	.11	.15**	.13	.13–.10
Independence-supportive behavior	.11**	.10**	.12**	.06	.10**	.09**	.07	.10	.08**	.11**	.07–.05
Dependence-supportive behavior	.58**	.28	.37**	.32**	.35**	.34**	.34**	.34**	.29**	.30**	.28–.24

*Significantly less than base probability ($p < .05$).
**Significantly more than base probability ($p < .05$).

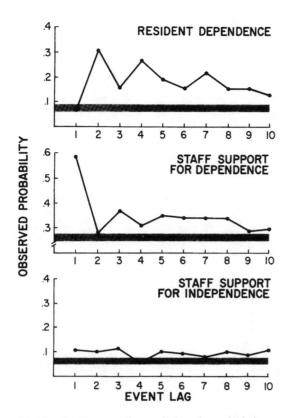

Figure 9. Base and conditional probability at 10 lags for three consequent behaviors following an instance of dependent behaviors of residents.

dent behavior stayed within base probability, which ranged from
.10 to .13.

Summary. The findings replicate and extend the results of
Study 3 as well as of the pilot study by Lester and Baltes (1978)
and work by Mikulic (1971). The following conclusions are offered.

First, as to base frequencies of resident and staff behaviors, it
is important to recognize that elderly residents exhibited a higher
level of independent behavior than dependent behavior, with independent acts exceeding dependent acts in a 1.4:1 ratio. Staff

behavior, on the other hand, demonstrated the reverse relationship. Staff showed far more dependence-supportive than independence-supportive behavior, with dependence-supportive acts being approximately four times as frequent.

Second, as to the interactional analysis focusing on the consequents of dependent and independent behavior by residents, the first major finding is that resident dependence was most frequently followed by dependence-supportive behavior of staff. Using operant perspectives, this finding can be interpreted as presenting a schedule of immediate and continuous staff reinforcement for dependent behavior by residents. When elderly residents showed independent self-maintenance behavior, however, nursing home staff exhibited a very low frequency of independence-supportive acts, not much beyond its low base probability. The putatively incongruous staff response to independence, dependence-supportive behavior, although occurring at a lower level than base probability rate and around a conditional probability of .20, was still the most frequent staff response: 3.3 times more frequent than independence-supportive behavior. Thus, residents could expect attention and reinforcement to be more likely forthcoming whenever they acted dependently rather than in an independent fashion. This consequence schedule for independent acts can be described as a DRO (differential reinforcement of other responses than the target response) schedule that should lead over time to a decrease in the target response. Thus, the same staff consequence delivered following two different and incompatible resident behaviors represents two structurally and functionally different contingency patterns.

Despite the apparent DRO schedule of staff behavior following independent behavior, independent behavior was still more frequent than dependent behavior (1.4:1). What maintains independent behaviors? Explaining this will require expansion of the behavior code to include recording of consequences from others than staff alone and a differentiation within the code of same category behavior into new and ongoing behaviors. Obviously, independent acts do not need the immediate presence of a social partner for reinforcement to occur but can be maintained by intrinsic or intermittent reinforcement schedules or both. In addition, they can be maintained by chaining; that is, each single behavior act is built into a chain of behaviors where each preceding behavior acts as stimulus control and each following behavior as reinforcement. As the data also suggest, social mediators in the form of staff have a constraining effect on independent behaviors. Thus, it seems likely that possible external reinforcement contingencies for resident independence are delivered by nonstaff social interactions. We will pick up this issue in the next studies.

Since the present study is a sequential-observational and the antecedent–consequent relationships temporal ones, causal properties cannot be assigned to the observed relationships. In concert, however, with the theoretical assumption that temporal association describes one of the sufficient conditions for causal inferences and with empirical evidence of the experimental operant findings, the present results are highly suggestive of a causal position. In conceptualizing dependence during morning care in elderly nursing home residents as being due in part to the nature of the social environment, the present outcome suggests that a major part of dependence is produced or maintained by nursing home staff behavior. Differential learning contingencies do exist in the social ecology of the nursing home for independent versus dependent behavior involving self-maintenance skills of elderly residents. These findings again suggest that, at least in the present nursing home setting, dependence does not appear as the outcome of non-contingent failure following independence and thus should not be associated with helplessness (Seligman, 1975).

The findings of Studies 3 and 4 justified systematic continuation and extension. They not only promised better understanding of dependence–independence in the older nursing home resident but also with the knowledge base requisite for effective intervention aimed at preventive optimization or corrective rehabilitation (see Study 14 by Baltes, Neumann, & Zank, 1994).

STUDY 5 (Baltes, Honn, Barton, Orzech, & Lago, 1983)

This study represents a major expansion of previous work in order to satisfy some of the suggestions noted in the earlier studies. First, time of observation was extended to involve the entire daytime for observations; second, three longitudinal occasions of measurement covering a 6-month period were implemented; third, elderly nursing home residents were stratified by length of institutionalization; fourth, the observation code was extended to include independent and dependent behaviors on the part of residents not only as they relate to self-care but also to other prosocial and asocial activities occurring during the day; and finally, an attempt was made to tap other social contingencies beyond those involving the nursing home staff.

Forty residents stratified by length of institutionalization (Group 1 = 2 to 12 months, Group 2 = 12 to 36 months, Group 3 = 48 to 60 months, and Group 4 = more than 84 months) and by gender ($N = 20$ each) were observed on three occasions: July, September, and December. Each occasion of measurement consisted of daily observations over a 14-day period. Residents were observed randomly each day with the restriction that each resident was observed during each hour of the day between 7 a.m. and 7 p.m., at least once during the 14 days.

For purposes of reliability assessment, the two observers of the day performed simultaneous observations on two randomly selected residents either at the beginning or the end of a daily circuit. Interobserver reliability was computed in two ways. First, Spearman rho correlations were calculated between two observers per occasion per resident behavior category. Averaged across the three occasions, these intercorrelations were .71 for constructively engaged, .76 for obstructively engaged, .74 for nonengaged, .91 for independent personal maintenance, and .90 for dependent personal maintenance behavior (for occasion 1 the five correlations are significant at the .005 level, for occasion 2 at the .05, and for occasion 3 at the .01 level).

Second, because such data are the focus of our research, interobserver reliability was computed not only at the level of single behavior frequency but on the level of behavior sequences. Thus, conditional probabilities were determined for all immediately subsequent behaviors (Lag 1) for each resident behavior and each occasion as well as across occasions. These behavior sequence profiles were compared for observers A and B via product-moment correlations separately for each of the five resident behaviors as criterion or antecedent behaviors. The correlations range in the .90s, indicating high interobserver reliability for interactional sequences (rather than single behavior frequencies) as well. Note that in both reliability computations we analyze sep-

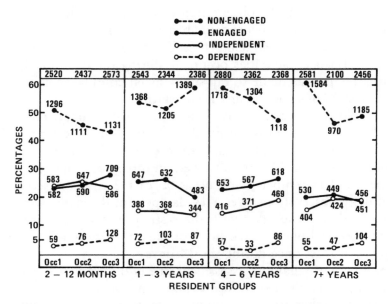

Figure 10. Percentages and frequencies of resident behaviors separately for the four groups and three occasions.

arately for each behavior, thus differentiating between low- and high-frequency behaviors.

Let us look at the results in three steps. First, we shall inspect the frequencies of elderly residents' behaviors, second the frequencies of the social partners' behaviors, and third the interactional behavior patterns involving elderly residents and their social partners.

When we inspect Figure 10 presenting the behavior of residents it is surprising that the observed frequencies of the five residents' behaviors show only small and insignificant differences between occasions within each group (see Figure 10). Temporal stability on the level of interindividual differences is generally high also. Of the 10 correlations between occasions 1 and 2 and 2 and 3, eight are significant ($p < .002$). Based on these findings we decided to collapse the data across the three occasions of measurement for each group (see Table 6; upper part). In terms of absolute frequencies across occasions and groups, a total of 27,721 behavioral instances of residents' behaviors was recorded.

Table 6. *Frequency and Percentage of Residents' and Social Partners' Behaviors Separately by Length of Institutionalization*

Behavioral Categories	Length of Institutionalization (months)				
	2–12	12–36	48–60	84+	Total
Resident					
Independent personal maintenance	1,673	1,088	1,218	1,252	5,231
	6.4	3.92	4.40	4.52	18.87
Dependent personal maintenance	254	249	169	162	834
	.92	.90	.61	.58	3.01
Nonengaged behaviors	3,201	3,861	3,987	3,342	14,391
	11.55	13.93	14.38	12.06	51.91
Constructively engaged	1,692	1,720	1,789	1,203	6,404
	6.10	6.20	6.45	4.34	23.10
Obstructively engaged	17	169	200	475	861
	.06	.61	.72	1.71	3.11
Total	6,837	7,087	7,363	6,434	27,721
	24.66	25.27	26.56	23.21	100.00
Social Partners					
Supportive of independence	44	60	42	26	172
	.89	1.21	.85	.53	3.48
Supportive of dependence	212	216	165	157	750
	4.29	4.37	3.34	3.18	15.18
Supportive of engagement	677	559	391	214	1,841
	13.70	11.31	7.91	4.33	37.25
No response	488	500	462	376	1,826
	9.87	10.12	9.85	7.61	36.95
Leaving	78	94	101	81	354
	1.58	1.90	2.04	1.64	7.16
Total	1,499	1,429	1,161	854	4,943
	30.33	28.91	23.49	17.29	100.00

Note: Sequential lag analyses consider only those resident behaviors that occur in the presence of social partners.

Of this total behavior pool 5,231 (19%) represented independent personal maintenance and 834 (3%) involved dependent personal maintenance behaviors; 6,404 (23%) were constructively engaged behaviors; 14,391 (52%) represent nonengaged behaviors, and 861 (3%) destructively engaged behaviors.

To examine the differences between groups and behavior categories of residents for statistical significance, an analysis of variance was used with length of institutionalization and behavior category as independent factors. Whereas differences between behavior categories are significant, differences between length of institutionalization are not.[1] Looking more specifically at behavior categories (using a posteriori *t* tests), we find nonengaged behavior to be significantly more frequent than all the other four behaviors; constructively engaged behavior and independent personal maintenance were significantly more frequent than the remaining two – obstructively engaged and dependent personal maintenance behaviors. When the data were subjected to a nonparametric analysis (Kruskal-Wallis), the same results were obtained. Figure 11 illustrates the findings for residents per group.

Looking again at Table 6 (lower part) we can inspect the behaviors of social partners per group and behavior category. A total of 4,943 behaviors of social partners were recorded across all three occasions and 40 residents. Here, too, an analysis of variance was performed to test for significances. As in the case of residents, findings indicate that differences between behavior categories are significant, but those between length of institutionalization are not. Specifically, no response and engagement-supportive behaviors are significantly more frequent than the remaining three behaviors of social partners; in addition, behavior supportive of dependent personal maintenance was significantly more frequent than the remaining two behaviors (leaving and independence-supportive self-care behavior). Figure 12 illustrates the findings for the behavior of staff separately for the four groups.

Of these observations, approximately 59% refer to staff and approximately 35% to fellow residents interacting with a focal resident; about 10% of the observations refer to resident–visitor or resident–volunteer worker interactions; the remaining 5% refer to resident–group interactions (see Figure 13).

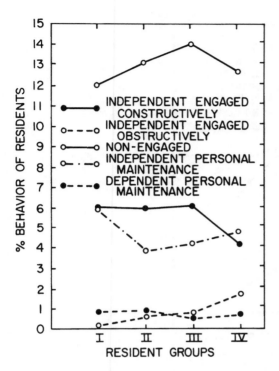

Figure 11. Distribution of resident behaviors separately for the four groups.

In a second step, we attend to the interaction patterns. Sequential lag analyses were computed per group, per occasion, per group across occasions, and across groups and occasions. Sequential behavior patterns looked nearly identical. We will, therefore, restrict our discussion to the overall sequential lag analyses (Lag 1 and Lag 2 data are shown in Table 7).

We will first focus on the consequent events of dependent personal maintenance behavior of residents as antecedent event (see Table 7). Residents' dependent behavior in the presence of social partners has a base probability of .03. Note first that this base rate is quite low. It is, for example, lower than that for residents' independent personal maintenance behavior (.16). Two consequent events depart from their base probability (with $p < .05$); dependence-supportive behavior by social partners and residents'

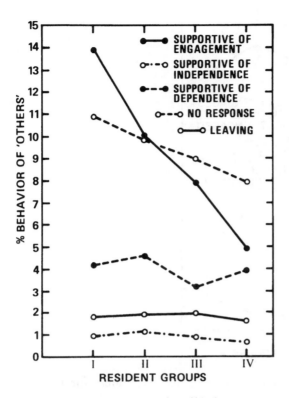

Figure 12. Distribution of staff behaviors separately for the four groups.

dependent personal maintenance behavior (see also Figure 14). Thus, the occurrence of dependent personal maintenance behaviors by residents has an effect on what behaviors social partners display. This effect is particularly obvious at Lag 1, when the conditional probability for the social partners' dependence-supportive behavior is .48 compared with its base rate of .02. There continues to be a statistically significant elevation in dependence-supportive behavior at all lags, with conditional probabilities ranging from .12 to .34 (see Figure 14). The criterion behavior itself, dependent personal maintenance behavior, is elevated also in the temporal flow subsequent to its occurrence, namely at Lags 2 and 4 (.40 and .32).

When inspecting the consequent events for independent personal maintenance behavior of residents, we can conclude the fol-

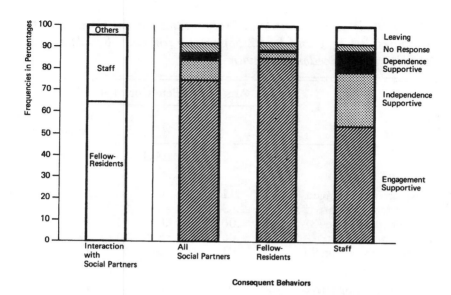

Figure 13. Distribution of behaviors across the different social partners.

lowing. Residents' independent personal maintenance behavior in the presence of others has a base probability of .16. The most frequent consequent event ($p < .05$) is a continuation of the residents' independent personal maintenance behaviors, showing conditional probabilities in the .50s and .60s. Independence-supportive behavior by social partners (base probability = .01) is not affected by the antecedent criterion behavior of residents' independence. Even the consequent probability of a diverging social behavior (i.e., dependence-supportive behavior) is neither reduced nor enhanced when elderly residents exhibit independent personal maintenance.

Turning now to constructively engaged behavior of residents we can see that for this criterion behavior, there are also two significantly increased behavior consequences: the behavior itself and engagement-supportive behavior by the social partner. As Figure 15 shows, for all five lags the conditional probabilities for residents' constructively engaged behavior following a previous instance of itself are significantly ($p < .05$) increased and range from .50 at Lag 1 to .64 at Lag 2 and remain in the .50s for the subsequent three lags. Engagement-supportive behavior by others

Table 7. *Base and Conditional Probabilities for All Consequent Behaviors at Lag 1 and Lag 2 Separately for Each Resident Behavior as Antecedent Behavior*

Consequent Behaviors	Antecedent Behavior of Residents					Base Probabilities
	1	2	3	4	5	
	LAG 1					
Resident						
Constructively engaged (1)	.50*	.12	.08	.03	.05	.19
Independent self-care (2)	.07	.63*	.02	.02	.04	.16
Dependent self-care (3)	.00	.00	.11*	.00	.01	.03
Nonengaged (4)	.06	.06	.02	.84*	.21	.44
Obstructively engaged (5)	.01	.01	.02	.01	.57*	.03
Social Partners						
Engagement-supportive	.23*	.05	.10*	.01	.03	.06
Dependence-supportive	.02	.02	.48*	.01	.02	.03
No response	.09	.08	.08	.07	.07	.06
	LAG 2					
Resident						
Constructively engaged (1)	.64*	.15	.13	.04	.06	.19
Independent self-care (2)	.10	.62*	.06	.03	.05	.16
Dependent self-care (3)	.02	.02	.39*	.01	.02	.03
Nonengaged (4)	.10	.10	.09	.86*	.21	.44
Obstructively engaged (5)	.01	.01	.01	.01	.59*	.03
Social Partners						
Supportive of engagement	.07	.05	.08	.01	.02	.06
Supportive of dependent self-care	.01	.01	.12*	.01	.02	.03
No response	.04	.03	.07	.03	.03	.06

Note. Two behaviors of social partners (independence-supportive self-care and leaving) are not included; their conditional probability never exceeded .03. Statistical significance is indicated only for those conditional probabilities exceeding .10.

*$p \leq .05$.

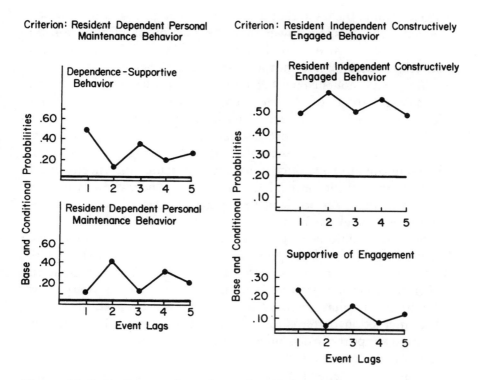

Figure 14 (left). Base and conditional probabilities for the two most likely events following dependent behavior of residents.
Figure 15 (right). Base and conditional probabilities for the two most likely events following constructively engaged behavior of residents.

(base probability = .06) shows conditional probabilities ($p < .05$) following resident constructively engaged behaviors ranging from a high of .23 at Lag 1 to a low of .07 at Lag 2. This outcome is another case for a convergence between the residents' and their social partners' action sequence.

There are two more behaviors of residents, obstructively engaged behavior and nonengaged behavior. Obstructively engaged behavior has a very low base probability (.03). The consequent behavior flow shows the behavior itself (i.e., obstructively engaged behavior) to be the most frequent ($p \le .05$) follow-up behavior for all lags, accounting for 60% of all behavioral consequences. Nonengaged behavior is the second most likely sequence at all lags, despite the fact that the conditional probabilities, which range in the .20s, are lower than the base probability of .44. As to social consequences or behaviors of the social partners, this criterion behavior does not appear to affect their action.

Residents' nonengaged behavior in the presence of others has a base probability of .44. Here again only one consequent behavior shows an increase beyond its base probability. Nonengaged behavior itself is the most frequent ($p < .05$), almost exclusive event following an instance of residents' nonengaged behaviors. Its conditional probability following a previous instance of itself rises above .80 for all five lags. Nonengaged behaviors by elderly residents, then, do not lead to a particular set of actions or reactions of social partners.

Several additional lag analyses were performed. First, we wanted to get rid of the possibility that the same behavior – i.e., independent behavior – can follow itself (autocorrelation). Therefore, event lags were determined under the condition that the criterion behavior could not be followed by itself at Lag 1. The interaction patterns just reported suggesting (1) continuous external support for dependent behavior, (2) intermittent external support for constructively engaged behavior, and (3) no external support for independent personal maintenance or for obstructively engaged or nonengaged behavior remain the same.

Second and third, when attempting to identify possible effects of organismic variables such as care status and sex of residents in the interaction patterns, we find quantitative differences in level of behavior between women and men and skilled and intermediate health care but only minor differences in interaction patterns. The latter differences are based, however, on relatively small samples and tentative statistical methodology and are less than impressive.

Summary. By extending the behavior code and observations across all times of the day and social partners other than staff, a more complete picture of both residents' as well as their social partners' behaviors in the nursing home context has been gained. Previous findings (Baltes et al., 1980; Barton et al., 1980) are strengthened by this study.

The first major finding of this replication and extension study is one of much similarity with and robustness of previous findings.

Additional times of day, varying length of institutionalization, increased number of behavior categories, as well as occasions of measurement and types of social partners did not alter the basic picture gained previously. We still find a relatively independent elderly resident who, however, is frequently nonengaged. We still find a social ecology, even though extended beyond staff, that shows more supportive behaviors of dependent personal maintenance than of independent personal maintenance. In addition, we find evidence for independence support by social partners, namely in the form of behaviors supportive of constructive engagement.

As to occasion of measurement, we find no significant differences between the three times of measurement in the four groups. Furthermore, the longitudinal stability of residents' behaviors appears to be high across the 6-month interval. This fact might be due to the time interval being too short to demonstrate behavior changes. Nevertheless, such an effect would have been expected in the group with the shortest institutionalization, given the frequent statement in the literature that major changes in residents take place during the first half year after institutionalization. Considering, however, that the four groups did not differ in mean age, range of age, nor health status, the lack of institutionalization effect becomes more understandable. The variation in length of institutionalization was cross-sectional. Thus, the samples may very well have been affected by selective survival or selective mortality. Only long-term longitudinal follow-ups can provide adequate information on the effect of institutionalization. Until then, we are impressed with the robustness of the present findings.

With regard to the *interaction patterns* between elderly residents and their social partners, the extension features did not alter the basic outcome but helped to differentiate the basic interaction patterns found in our previous studies. Independent personal maintenance behaviors of residents continue to find little attention from the social ecology, even if social partners other than staff are considered. They cluster in chains, which may mean a sequence of a variety of independent behaviors or the same independent behavior extended over a long time period.

Constructively engaged behavior does receive intermittent support from social partners. A resident who is involved in prosocial behaviors not only continues to be prosocial but intermittently experiences positive attention from social partners for such behavior. This discrepant finding for the two independence-related behaviors suggests that they function differently in terms of setting the stage (stimulus control) for social interaction. It appears important to maintain such a differentiation in the observational code in future work.

Dependent personal maintenance behaviors are followed consistently by dependence-supportive behaviors from social partners. Dependent behaviors obviously act as prompts for social partners to behave in a congruent fashion, namely supportive of dependence. In contrast, when residents exhibit nonengaged behaviors there is no reaction (supportive or nonsupportive) from the social ecology. For whatever reasons, nonengaged behaviors appear to possess no direct information for action by others. As is true for the case of independence, it appears necessary to differentiate between these two types of dependence-related behaviors (i.e., dependent personal maintenance and nonengagement); they exhibit different social interaction patterns that need explication in future work. The robustness of the interaction patterns is highlighted in this study in that health status, gender, and other person-variables do not seem to have an impact on the interaction patterns.

In conclusion, the present findings corroborate earlier data on the discrepant social ecologies for independent and dependent behavior of the elderly resident. The extension of the social ecology to include social partners other than staff did not alter the interactional patterns. A congruent interaction pattern for dependent behavior remains. For independent personal maintenance behaviors, consistently strong contingencies from social partners are still missing. Our data show that these independent behaviors are clustered in chains. *Chaining* is a term used in operant-learning theory and this pattern has been shown to maintain behavior, in this case, independent personal maintenance behavior. Unfortunately, the data of Study 5 do not allow us to discern different events within the same category a posteriori. We do not know whether the clustering means a continuation of the same independent behavior or whether the clustering consists of a chain of different independent acts. This issue will be addressed in the next study.

The extension of the two categories of dependence- and independence-related behaviors to include behaviors other than self-care proved useful. The present findings show that neither domain is a single homogeneous class. With respect to independence, the present findings indicate a differentiation between interactional patterns related to independent personal maintenance and those related to constructively and obstructively engaged behaviors. The difference between the positive social contingencies (for constructively engaged behaviors) and zero contingency (for independent personal maintenance behaviors) is important from an ecological viewpoint. This differential social reaction seems to speak to expected role-behavior congruencies of residents and staff in institutions (Goffman, 1960). With respect to dependence, a differentiation between patterns related to dependent and nonengaged behaviors seems necessary as well.

We have argued before that the regularity of specific and systematic social consequences of dependent behaviors and the lack thereof for independent behaviors, as seen in the present nursing home studies, determine a situation contrary to that apt to produce learned helplessness. The finding is one of contingency, not one of noncontingency. Our description of dependency is also different from Rodin and Langer's (1977) discussion of lack of control. Rodin and Langer (1977), Langer (1979), and Langer and Rodin (1976), using a cognitive approach, have argued that real or expected experiences of physical deficiencies and of social prejudices lead the elderly person to perceive a lack of control over his or her environment which, in turn, leads to dependency in the sense of learned helplessness. We would argue that our data suggest that dependent behaviors, even if resulting from loss of control, can be instrumental. If dependency is followed by a systematic contingency, a person engaging in dependent behavior will set the occasion for that contingency to occur and, therefore, will control the environment. It appears necessary to gain a clearer understanding of the differences between types of dependent and independent behaviors and their consequences before we label a dependent elderly person as helpless or out of control (Baltes & Skinner, 1983).

STUDY 6 (Baltes, Kindermann, & Reisenzein, 1986)

This study, while addressing the same issues as the previous studies, provided additional information relevant for a *cross-cultural comparison,* in that the study was conducted in a nursing home in Berlin, Germany.

The study is an exact replica of Study 5, with a sample of 39 residents stratified into three groups of length of institutionalization ($N = 13$ each; Group 1 < 1 year, Group 2 = 1 to 3 years, and Group 3 > 3 years) and 20 staff members, all visitors, volunteer workers (these latter two categories made up only a handful of people), and fellow residents. Because of the large data set in this study, we were able to examine more closely the effect of such factors as gender, age, and length of institutionalization on the interaction patterns. The results are presented in two parts. First, we shall describe the frequency distribution of the behaviors separately for the elderly and their social partners. Second, the interactional behavior patterns involving the target residents and their social partners will be looked at.

Let us first look at Table 8 and the behavior profiles. A summary of the frequencies and proportions of all behaviors is presented in Table 8 separately for the three groups of residents (length of institutionalization). As can be seen, a total of 45,441 behavioral acts were recorded during the 21 days of observation.

Considering the behavior of residents, a total of 32,469 instances of behaviors of target residents were observed. Constructively engaged behavior was by far the most frequent one with 16,236 instances (or 50%), followed by independent self-care behaviors (8,591, or 26%), and nonengaged behaviors (6,805, or 21%). Finally, destructively engaged behaviors were observed 549 times (1.7%) and dependent self-care behaviors 297 times (0.9%).

A total of 12,972 instances of behaviors of social partners were recorded. Of these, *no response* represents the most frequently observed behavior with 7,617 instances (59%), followed by engagement-supportive behavior (4,286 or 33%), independence-supportive behaviors (374, 2.9%), dependence-supportive behaviors (366, 2.8%), and leaving (267, 2.1%). Finally, behavior supportive of nonengagement was observed only 62 times (0.5%).

Figure 16 gives an overview of the distribution of these behaviors across the different social partners. Approximately 85% of the behaviors recorded are behaviors of fellow residents and only 5% are staff (the remaining 10% depict the behavior of other social partners such as volunteer workers, visitors, and groups).

Table 8. *Frequency and Percentage of Behaviors Separately for Residents and Social Partners by Years of Institutionalization*

Behavior Categories	Length of Institutionalization (years)			
	0–1	1–3	>3	Total
Residents				
Constructively engaged behaviors	51.6 5,621	53.4 5,593	45.2 5,022	50.0 16,236
Destructively engaged behaviors	1.2 132	2.4 249	1.4 159	1.7 540
Nonengaged behaviors	24.9 2,722	16.1 1,688	21.5 2,395	20.7 6,805
Independent self-care behaviors	21.6 2,353	27.2 2,846	30.5 3,392	26.3 8,591
Dependent self-care behaviors	0.6 61	0.9 89	1.3 147	0.9 297
Sum	100 10,889	100 10,465	100 11,115	100 32,469
Social partners				
Engagement-supportive behaviors	37.8 1,502	28.2 1,206	32.3 1,578	33.0 4,286
Nonengagement-supportive behaviors	0.2 9	0.4 15	0.8 38	0.5 62
Independence-supportive behaviors	2.6 105	1.4 59	4.3 210	2.9 374
Dependence-supportive behaviors	1.9 76	2.8 116	3.6 174	2.8 366
No response	54.9 2,184	64.4 2,662	56.8 2,771	58.7 7,617
Leaving	2.4 96	1.7 73	2.2 107	2.1 267
Sum	100 3,972	100 4,131	100 4,878	100 12,972
Sum total	14,861	14,596	15,993	45,441

No response is the most frequent behavior exhibited by fellow residents. In contrast, staff members seem to exhibit more differential as well as more active behaviors (see Figure 16).

To test for the significance of these differences, the data for residents and staff were subjected to a 3 (Length of Institutionalization) $\times$ 11 (Behavior Categories) $\times$ 3 (Time of Day of Observation) analysis of covariance with Age as a covariate.[2] As in the previous study, differences between behavior categories were significant; constructively engaged behaviors of residents and no response of staff were the most frequent followed by engagement-supportive behaviors of staff as well as nonengaged behaviors of residents. Length of institutionalization had no main effect and only a negligible and unsystematic effect on some specific behaviors.

The second step in the data analysis involved, as always, the examination of sequential interactional patterns between residents and their social partners. The focus here, as in the previous studies, is foremost on the consequences of the behaviors of residents.

Table 9 provides an overview of the results of the sequential lag analysis for Lags 1 and 2, separately for each resident behavior category as antecedent. It should be noted that only those resident behaviors that were observed in the presence of social partners were included in the lag analysis. Of the total of 32,469 resident behaviors, 26,518 (or 81.6%) were observed in the presence of social partners.

Using the behaviors of the target residents as antecedent events, lags were computed first without any restrictions as to the consequent events (see Table 9). The same analysis was then repeated, with the restriction that at Lag 1 the antecedent behavior could not be followed by itself. This procedure corrects for autocorrelations. Third, to examine possible effects of variables such as sex, age, length of institutionalization as well as type of social partners on the interaction patterns, separate lag analyses were performed for these subgroups. Finally, to obtain data on the reciprocity of the interaction patterns, lag analyses involving the behaviors of social partners as antecedents were also computed.

Because this study is a cross-cultural replica of Study 5, let me summarize and compare the interactional patterns only with re-

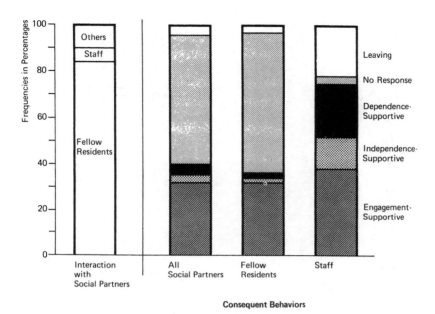

Figure 16. Distribution of behaviors across types of social partner.

gard to Lag 1 and Lag 2, rather than reporting the results in great detail. Basically, the data support and confirm the previously found interaction patterns, with a clear dominance of dependence-supportive behaviors over independence-supportive behaviors. In the context of dependent self-care behaviors dependence-supportive behavior of social partners were significantly elevated, no response was significantly decreased. The most probable consequent events for independent self-care behavior were no response from social partners or more of the same.

Constructively engaged behavior, which had the highest base probability (.35) of all behaviors of residents, had three significantly enhanced consequent behaviors: engagement-supportive behavior and, at least as probable, no response of social partners as well as a continuation of the antecedent behavior itself from Lag 2 on. Obstructively engaged behavior of residents was most likely followed by no response and engagement-supportive behavior of social partners, the latter albeit only in Lag 1. The con-

Table 9. *Base and Conditional Probabilities for All Consequent Behaviors at Lag 1 and Lag 2 Separately with Residents' Behaviors as Antecedent Behaviors*

	Antecedent Behaviors					
Consequent Behaviors	Constructively Engaged Behavior 01	Destructively Engaged Behavior 02	Nonengaged Behavior 03	Independent Self-care 04	Dependent Self-care 05	Base Probabilities
			LAG 1			
Resident						
01	.29	.06	.12	.08	.07	.35
02	.00	.19*	.00	.00	.00	.01
03	.03	.03	.82*	.01	.01	.13
04	.03	.03	.02	.34*	.09	.17
05	.00	.00	.00	.00	.06*	.01
Social Partner						
06	.28*	.20*	.02	.04	.07	.11
08	.00	.00	.00	.05*	.05*	.01
09	.01	.00	.00	.01	.58*	.01
10	.34*	.44*	.00	.45*	.04	.19
11	.01	.01	.00	.01	.04*	.01

LAG 2

Resident					
01	.59*	.17	.10	.08	.16	.35
02	.01	.46*	.00	.00	.00	.01
03	.04	.04	.72*	.01	.04	.13
04	.05	.06	.02	.50*	.19	.17
05	.01	.00	.00	.01	.40*	.01

Social Partners					
06	.07	.04	.05	.04	.04	.11
08	.00	.00	.00	.01	.02	.01
09	.00	.00	.00	.01	.05*	.01
10	.23*	.22*	.10	.32*	.05*	.19
11	.00	.00	.00	.01	.00	.01

*$p < .05$.

ditional probability of obstructively engaged behavior following a previous instance of itself was also significantly increased at all lags. It should be noted here that fellow residents' behavior was most often coded as "no response."

Nonengaged behavior of residents was observed in the presence of social partners with a base probability of .13. A continuation of the same behavior was the most frequently observed consequence. It is also noteworthy that nonengaged behavior as antecedent event inhibits significantly the occurrence of *all* other behaviors including those of social partners.

When excluding the possibility that a behavior can follow itself in Lag 1 (i.e., the most immediate event for independent behavior is another independent behavior) results remained essentially unchanged for independent behaviors as antecedent. That is, no response by social partners and a continuation of the antecedent behavior (from Lag 2 on) remained the most frequent consequent events. It should also be noted that the no response result was nearly exclusively due to behaviors of fellow residents. Independence-supportive behaviors as well as dependence-supportive behaviors showed significant conditional probabilities as consequent events but occurred at extremely small frequencies. No interpretation is possible, therefore.

When using the same restriction in the re-analysis of the behavioral stream following nonengaged behaviors, we find constructively engaged behaviors of residents as a significantly enhanced consequent event; from Lag 2 on, two behaviors of social partners, namely no response and engagement-supportive behavior and nonengaged behavior itself are significantly enhanced consequent events.

In Study 6 we also looked at interaction patterns separately for gender, length of institutionalization, and care status. Since we had larger groups in Study 6 than in Study 5, lag analyses involving behaviors of residents as antecedents were performed separately for male and female residents, for the three groups of residents who differed in length of institutionalization, as well as those who received intermediate versus skilled nursing care. While a statistical test of group comparisons between lag sequential patterns is currently not available, it is evident when inspecting the data that the interaction patterns do not differ in any essential way from the ones reported previously (see findings for gender and care status in Figure 17).

The findings of the lag analyses involving behavior of social partners as antecedents are shown in Table 10 and can be briefly summarized in two parts: First, the dependence-supportive, independence-supportive, and engagement-supportive behaviors of social partners are followed most likely in Lag 1 by the *complementary* behaviors of residents. Thus, engagement-supportive behavior is followed most likely by constructively engaged behavior of residents; dependence-supportive behavior is followed most likely by dependent personal maintenance behavior; and independence-supportive behavior is followed most likely by independent personal maintenance behavior (conditional probabilities at Lag 1 are .82, .55, and .69, respectively). Second, the behaviors leaving and no response of social partners are followed most typically by independent self-care behavior as well as constructively engaged or obstructively engaged behavior of residents. In addition, nonengaged behaviors of residents emerged as a significantly decreased consequent event following no response.

In summary, comparing the results of the present study with those of our American studies, we find, in general, high agreement between the *interactional patterns* observed in both cultural settings, that is, the nursing homes in West Berlin and in Pennsylvania. Discrepancies in the data are found mainly on the level of frequencies and thus are quantitative rather than qualitative in nature.

Residents in both homes exhibit a fair amount of independent personal maintenance behavior (26% and 19%). Residents in both settings exhibit fairly low frequencies of dependent personal maintenance behavior (9% versus 3%). It should be emphasized that the lower frequency of dependent behaviors in the Berlin home must be considered a very conservative estimate. Because of different cultural customs, the same observational procedure turned out to be more obtrusive in the Berlin home, causing many of the dependent self-care contexts to be hidden from our observations.

Larger differences occurred, however, with regard to the observed frequencies of nonengaged as well as constructively en-

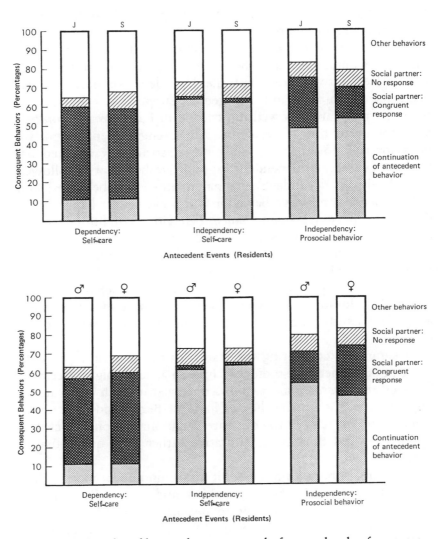

Figure 17. Results of lag analyses separately for two levels of care status and for men and women.

gaged behaviors between the German and American samples. In the German study we find nonengaged behaviors only 21% of the time, compared to, for instance, 52% in the American study by Baltes et al. (1983). Conversely, constructively engaged behaviors were much more frequently observed in the Berlin nursing home

(50%) than in the Pennsylvania nursing home (23%). In sum, the nursing home resident in Berlin exhibited a more active picture than the one in Pennsylvania.

Looking at the frequency distribution of the behaviors of social partners, it must be mentioned first that in the Berlin nursing home fellow residents were the most frequently observed social partners, accounting for 85% of the behaviors versus 5% for staff. In contrast, in the American nursing home fellow residents and staff each accounted for about 50% of the behaviors of social partners (Baltes et al., 1983). This striking difference between the American and the German nursing home regarding the makeup of observed social partnerships could explain some of the discrepancies in the frequency distribution of their behaviors.

The main differences between the two settings in the frequencies of the behaviors of social partners concern no response and independence-supportive behavior. No response was by far the most frequently observed behavior of social partners in this German study (59%), whereas it accounted for only 37% of behaviors in the study by Baltes et al. (1983). This difference is due to the fellow residents. When differentiating between staff and fellow residents, no response is shown most often by fellow residents, less often by staff. Conversely, in the case of dependence-supportive behavior, which was observed far less frequently in the nursing home in West Berlin than in the nursing home in Pennsylvania (2.8% vs. 15%), we see that such behavior is almost exclusively performed by staff. Within staff behavior, dependence-supportive behavior makes up 22% of all behaviors.

Thus, the observed differences between the American and the German nursing home regarding the frequency distribution of social partners' behaviors may be explained by taking into account the large differences in the composition of the social partnerships, and the observed differences between the behavior profiles of staff and fellow residents. Note that the rather small contribution of staff behavior to the total number of interactions with residents in the Berlin home also results in a less differentiated and less active social environment for the residents.

As alluded to previously, this frequency difference did not result in differences concerning the interaction patterns. As in the American home, we again found the following.

Table 10. Base and Conditional Probabilities for All Consequent Behaviors at Lag 1 and Lag 2 Separately with Social Partners' Behaviors as Antecedent Behaviors

	Antecedent Behaviors				
Consequent Behaviors	Engagement-supportive Behavior 06	Independence-supportive Behavior 08	Dependence-supportive Behavior 09	No Response 10	Base Probabilities
			LAG 1		
Resident					
01	.82*	.20	.22	.57*	.35
02	.02*	.01	.00	.02*	.01
03	.05	.02	.03	.03	.13
04	.11	.69*	.19	.37*	.17
09	.00	.06*	.55*	.00	.01

LAG 2

Resident					
01	.23	.10	.14	.45*	.35
02	.01	.00	.00	.02*	.01
03	.04	.01	.02	.07	.13
04	.05	.15	.10	.29*	.17
05	.00	.02	.05*	.00	.01
Social Partners					
06	.50*	.20*	.12	.04	.11
08	.02*	.35*	.04*	.00	.01
09	.01	.05*	.36*	.01	.01
10	.11	.05	.09	.11	.19
11	.02*	.04*	.08*	.01	.01

Note: Behavior category *Leaving* (11) as an antecedent event is not included in this table because all its consequent events are scored as "asocial" and thus are not included in the lag analyses.

*p < .01

1. Independent self-maintenance behavior is followed most typically by no response from social partners.
2. Dependent self-care behavior is followed most typically by dependence-supportive behaviors of social partners.
3. Constructively engaged behavior of residents is only intermittently followed by engagement-supportive behavior of social partners.
4. Obstructively engaged and nonengaged behaviors, similar to independent self-maintenance behavior, are typically ignored by the social environment.

Thus, we find again that dependent behaviors, despite their low base frequency, are better instruments for securing social contact than any other behaviors.

The present data also corroborate our previous findings that indicate a considerable robustness of the interaction patterns. That is, the basic structure of the interaction patterns is not influenced by factors such as residents' age, sex, or length of institutionalization. It should be pointed out, however, that the observational studies conducted so far have all been cross-sectional rather than longitudinal. Thus, the conclusions regarding possible effects of length of institutionalization and age must be considered as only tentative, due to problems such as selective survival or selective mortality. A more adequate assessment of the possible effects of institutionalization requires a longitudinal study.

The present data also confirm the reciprocal interaction patterns when considering the behavior of social partners as antecedents. Residents show the respective *complementary* behaviors as the most likely consequences.

In conclusion, two observations can be made. First, the divergent interactional patterns involving independent versus dependent self-care behavior, identified in previous American studies, were replicated in the German nursing home setting. Here, too, dependent self-care behaviors turn out to control desirable social consequences: social attention and contact. Second, the findings support the notion, introduced earlier, that dependent behavior is not necessarily due to learned helplessness. On the basis of our present data, we have to conclude that the nursing home does not represent an environment characterized by noncontingency. On the contrary, it appears that the nursing home environment is characterized by unambiguous and differential contingencies. Thus, at least as far as we can judge from the objective contingencies, dependent behavior does not seem to constitute an instance of lack of control or helplessness; in fact, it appears to be resourceful, even pragmatic behavior. But of course, it can be argued that objective contingency is not the only and perhaps not even the most important factor that determines an individual's sense of control (Baltes & Skinner, 1983).

Two questions seem particularly pressing; one refers to the functional property of the interaction patterns and the other to the issue of the cause of these patterns. Do we witness an age or an institution effect or both? These considerations, when taken together, suggest to us two avenues for future research. On the one hand, a more fine-grained analysis of the functional role of dependent behaviors in the elderly should be conducted. This will require further differentiation and refinement of the current behavioral coding scheme, as well as the implementation of additional measurement strategies (e.g., collection of self-report data). On the other hand, the effects of age versus institutionalization need to be disentangled.

STUDY 7 (Baltes, Kindermann, Reisenzein, & Schmid, 1987)

This study picks up on questions raised by Studies 5 and 6. Thus, the focus is on three major objectives:

1. To identify more closely the functional properties of the observed behavioral contingencies by coding not only type but also dyadic form of behavior exhibited by residents and social partners
2. To analyze the hypothesis that independent behaviors are maintained by chaining, an issue that was addressed by coding each behavior as either continuous or discontinuous
3. To test the generalizability of these and previous findings by extending the target population to include a sample of elderly persons in a home for chronically ill

We did not expect differences in the basic nature of the interaction patterns, as care status in our previous studies had not shown an effect on interaction patterns. Therefore, our expectation was that with chronically ill elderly persons, the interaction patterns found in nursing homes would only be magnified, because dependence-related behaviors would be more frequent in the home for chronically ill.

Since we compared two quite different homes whose residents might exhibit quite different levels of health status, which could have an impact on dependency-related behaviors of residents as well as staff, we checked for health status. Instead of examining health problems as recorded in residents' charts, however, we collected mortality data two years after the observations took place. We hypothesized that mortality rates should be higher in the home with a lower health status of the residents. The mortality data support our expectation in that significantly more residents had died in the home for the chronically ill (24 persons of 39) than in the nursing home (8 persons of 39).

Expressed differently, after 2 years 31 of the 39 nursing home residents were still alive compared to 15 of the 39 chronically ill elderly. Thus, we should expect a difference in the magnitude of dependence-related behaviors in the home for the chronically ill. Looking at the observational findings, let us begin by inspecting the behavioral frequencies and then the interactional patterns again.

As in the descriptions of the preceding studies, we turn first to the behavior profiles. The relative frequencies observed for type of behavior of the target residents are displayed in the left half of Figure 18, separately for two settings (nursing home in the upper part and home for the chronically ill in the lower part). A total of 23,547 behavioral events were observed: 10,104 in the nursing home and 13,443 in the home for chronically ill. Overall the most frequent behavior observed was constructively engaged behavior (50% and 45%, respectively), followed by independent self-care behavior (38% and 29%). Nonengaged behavior ranked third (4% and 10%), followed by dependent self-care behavior (3% and 5%) and destructively engaged behavior (3% and 1%).

As to the behavior frequencies of social partners, a total of 4,188 behaviors were recorded: 2,013 in the nursing home and 2,175 in the home for chronically ill. Figure 18 (right half) shows the highest percentage in both settings for engagement-supportive behaviors (68% and 45%, respectively, in the nursing home and

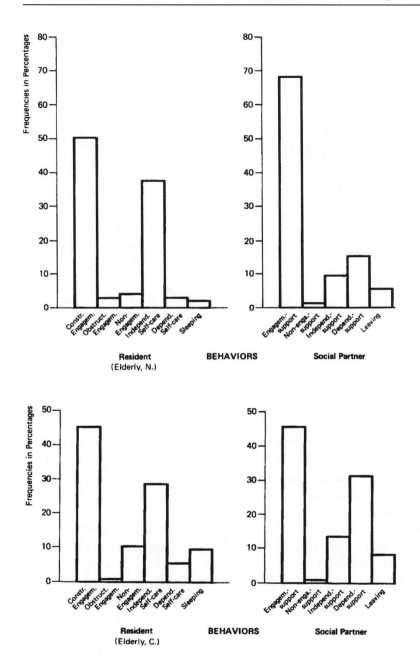

Figure 18. Frequencies of observed behaviors for residents and staff in a nursing home (upper part) and a home for chronically ill (lower part).

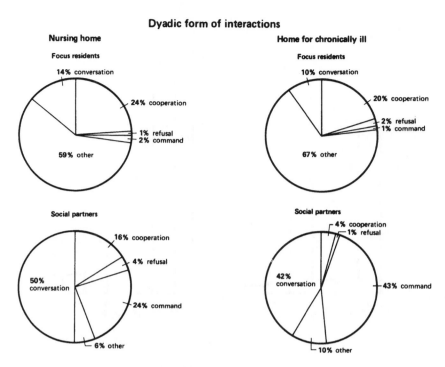

Figure 19. Frequencies of dyadic form of behavior for residents and staff in two homes.

the home for chronically ill) followed by dependence-supportive behaviors (15% and 32%). The third most frequent category refers to independence-supportive behaviors (10% and 14%), followed by leaving (6% and 8%) and nonengagement-supportive behaviors (each 1%).

Now, remember objective 1 of Study 7 was to include the dyadic form of behavior. Figure 19 (upper two circles) shows the relative frequencies of the form categories of the behaviors of target residents, separately for each setting. Note that due to the narrow definitions of the form categories, the *miscellaneous other* category is the most frequent. Because this category is of no importance to us, it will not be considered any further. Among the remaining five categories, compliance/cooperation ranks highest in both settings (14% and 20%), followed by conversation (14% and 10%). In third place, but much less frequent, is suggestion/request/command (2% and 1%), followed by refusal/resistance

(1% and 2%). Intention is a very infrequent form category for resident behaviors in both homes and is not included in the figure.

When looking at the form categories of the behaviors of social partners (Figure 19, lower circles), the most frequent form category is conversation (50% and 42%) followed by suggestion/request/command (24% and 43%) and compliance/cooperation (16% and 4%). In fourth place is refusal/resistance (4% and 1%).

To test the differences between the two homes with regard to type and form of the observed behaviors, a 2 × 11 × 6 (Institution × Type of Behavior × Form of Behavior) analysis of variance was computed.[3] Results indicate significant differences were enhanced by the setting. Remember, it was expected that in the home for the chronically ill, dependence-related behaviors both for residents and social partners would be observed more often, whereas in the nursing home, independence-related behaviors were expected to be higher. Moreover, regardless of type of behavior, it was expected that in the home for the chronically ill, the more passive forms would characterize the behavior of the residents and the more active forms the behavior of social partners. In contrast, in the nursing home we expected more active forms of behavior.

These hypotheses were partly supported by the findings. Results favoring the home for the chronically ill were found in the case of dependence-related behaviors for sleeping and nonengaged behaviors of residents. Of the independence-related behaviors, constructively engaged behavior of residents and engagement-supportive behavior of social partners in the form of suggestion/command, compliance/cooperation, and refusal are significantly more frequent in the nursing home. Dependent and independent self-care behaviors of residents just miss significance, whereas dependence-supportive and independence-supportive behaviors of social partners do not show any significant differences between the two homes.

Objective 2 of Study 7 was to investigate the continuity or discontinuity of behaviors appearing in strings or chains (see Table 11). When comparing continuity versus discontinuity for type of behavior of residents, we were mostly interested in independent self-care behaviors. A chi-square statistic was used to test the differences between old (continuous) and new (discontinuous) behaviors for this behavior category. The results show that independent self-care behaviors are significantly more often coded as

Table 11. *Frequencies of Discontinuous and Continuous Behaviors of Elderly Residents in Two Settings, the Nursing Home and the Home for the Chronically Ill*

| | | Continuity of Behavior | | |
Type of Behavior	Category Change	Same Behavior/ Same Category	New Behavior/ Same Category	Total
Sleeping	26	170	2	198
	(162)	(1,152)	(0)	(1,314)
Constructively engaged	2,514	1,457	1,125	5,096
	(2,858)	(2,030)	(1,195)	(6,083)
Destructively engaged	166	106	38	310
	(67)	(11)	(2)	(80)
Nonengaged	189	211	3	403
	(448)	(920)	(11)	(1,379)
Independent self-care	1,641	1,206	958	3,805
	(1,899)	(987)	(981)	(3,867)
Dependent self-care	290	0	2	292
	(700)	(0)	(20)	(720)
Sum	4,826	3,150	2,128	10,104
	(6,134)	(5,100)	(2,209)	(13,443)

Note: Numbers in parentheses refer to the home for the chronically ill.

new or discontinuous in both settings. Thus, the assumption of chaining seems to be a possible explanatory principle for the maintenance of independent self-care behaviors. Chaining in the operant learning model refers to a sequence of behaviors performed by the same person, in which each act is both a discriminative stimulus for the subsequent event and a reinforcing stimulus for the preceding one. Once the sequence is started it will continue to the last event in the chain, which itself might be followed by an external reinforcer.

Objective 3 was to look at interaction sequences examining type and form of behavior. Several different sequential lag analyses were performed with the present data. To permit a comparison of the present results to those of the previous studies, lag analyses were computed first with type of resident behaviors as antecedent events. Second, type and form categories were combined as antecedent events. Third, lag analyses were performed with the behaviors of social partners as antecedents both for type alone and for type and form of behaviors combined. All analyses included only data sets in which both partners were present and could be coded. This means that out of the total of 23,547 behaviors of residents, 21,316 (8,387 in Setting 1 and 12,929 in Setting 2) were coded with a social partner present. Behaviors of social partners were observed only in the presence of a resident, 2,013 in Setting 1 and 2,175 in Setting 2. Thus, the lag analyses were based on a total of 10,400 behavioral events in Setting 1 and 15,104 events in Setting 2. All analyses were performed separately for the two settings. Table 12 shows all consequent events in Lag 1 for the nursing home setting separately for the behavior of residents and social partners as antecedents.

Let's first look at dependent behavior of residents as the antecedent event. When looking at the behavioral flow following the occurrence of dependent self-care behavior, the most likely consequent event is dependence-supportive behavior of social partners. Its conditional probabilities in both settings in Lag 1 amount to .31 and .62, respectively. When one considers type and form together, the most frequent combination, dependent self-care as compliance/cooperation (accounting for more than 80% of all dependent self-care behaviors), is most likely followed by dependence-supportive behaviors of social partners in the form of suggestion/request/command.

Turning to independent self-care behaviors as antecedents, they are most likely followed by more of the same behavior of residents with conditional probabilities of .60 in Setting 1 and .55 in Setting 2. Thus, independent self-care behaviors are most likely to occur in bouts or chains. In addition, independent self-care behaviors are also followed by both dependence-supportive (.04) and independence-supportive (.04) behaviors of social partners.

Using the information from lag analyses of type and form of behavior combined, one finds that the only significant interaction pattern in Lag 1 is for independent self-care as compliance/cooperation (which makes for about 40% of all independent behaviors) in both settings. This antecedent event is followed significantly by more of the same behavior of residents (.65 in Setting 1 and .56 in Setting 2).

Table 12. *Base and Conditional Probabilities for All Consequent Events at Lag 1 Separately for Each Antecedent Event in the Nursing Home Setting*

	Consequent Event										
	Resident's Behavior						Social Partner's Behavior				
Antecedent Event	00	01	02	03	04	05	06	07	08	09	11
Target Resident											
00 Sleeping	.95*	.05	.00	.00	.00	.00	.00	.00	.00	.00	.00
01 Constructively engaged	.00	.51*	.01	.03	.13	.00	.28*	.00	.01	.02	.01
02 Destructively engaged	.00	.14	.39*	.03	.08	.00	.29*	.02	.01	.01	.03
03 Nonengaged	.00	.31	.02	.57*	.05	.00	.03	.00	.01	.01	.00
04 Independent self-care	.00	.23	.01	.00	.60*	.00	.05	.00	.04*	.04*	.02
05 Dependent self-care	.00	.15	.00	.00	.38*	.01	.03	.00	.09	.31*	.03
Social Partner											
06 Engagement-supportive	.00	.77*	.04	.00	.18	.00	.00	.00	.00	.00	.00
07 Nonengagement-supportive	.00	.83*	.09	.00	.09	.00	.00	.00	.00	.00	.00
08 Independence-supportive	.00	.10	.01	.00	.78*	.09	.00	.00	.00	.02	.00
09 Dependence-supportive	.00	.04	.00	.00	.19	.76*	.00	.00	.00	.00	.00
11 Leaving	.00	.30	.04	.00	.56*	.00	.06	.01	.02	.01	.00
Base probability	.01	.41	.02	.03	.30	.03	.13	.00	.02	.03	.01

Note: A total of 10,400 behaviors in the presence of social partners (8,387 behaviors of residents and 2,013 behaviors of social partners) were observed.
$*p < .01$ and $N > 50$.

Examining the consequences of constructively engaged behavior, the most likely consequent event following constructively engaged behaviors in both settings in Lag 1 is more of the same behavior (.51 in Setting 1 and .57 in Setting 2). The second most likely event for both settings is engagement-supportive behavior of social partners (.28 in Setting 1 and .16 in Setting 2).

Considering the results for type and form of behavior combined, constructively engaged behavior in the form of conversation (more than 20% of all constructively engaged behaviors in both settings), is followed closely by engagement-supportive behaviors in the form of conversation (.61 in Setting 1 and .53 in Setting 2).

Finally, nonengaged and destructively engaged behavior and sleeping were found for the most part to stimulate no reactions in social partners. More specifically, the only significant consequent events following these behaviors were more behaviors from the same behavior class, except for destructively engaged behaviors in Setting 1. In this case, they are also followed by engagement-supportive behaviors from social partners (conditional probability .29).

Reversing our perspective of the behavioral stream the behaviors of social partners – dependence-, independence-, and engagement-supportive behavior and leaving – are considered as antecedent events. All behaviors of the social partners are followed by the complementary behavior of residents (see Table 12). Consequently, dependence-supportive behaviors are followed most likely in Lag 1 by dependent self-care behavior of residents (conditional probabilities are in the high .70s for both settings), independence-supportive behaviors by independent self-care behaviors of residents (conditional probabilities are .78 and .79, respectively, in Settings 1 and 2), engagement-supportive behavior by constructively engaged behavior of residents (conditional probabilities are .77 and .79, respectively).

When considering type and form combined, we find that dependence-supportive behaviors in the form of suggestion/request/command (more than 80% of all dependence-supportive behaviors in both settings) are followed most likely by dependent self-care behaviors in the form of compliance/cooperation (conditional probabilities are more than .80 in both settings).

Independence-supportive behavior as suggestion/request/command (91% of all independence-supportive behaviors in the home for the chronically ill and 68% in the nursing home) is followed most likely by independent self-care behavior in the form of compliance/cooperation (.79 and .72, respectively, in Setting 1 and Setting 2); engagement-supportive behavior as conversation (the most frequent combination of engagement-supportive behaviors with 72% in the nursing home and 93% in the home for the chronically ill) is followed most likely by constructively engaged behavior in the form of conversation (.58 in Setting 1 and .62 in Setting 2). Leaving of social partners is followed in both settings most likely by independent self-care behaviors of residents (.56 and .46).

In summary, and as expected, the behavior profiles of residents and social partners in the two homes observed in the present study show both similarity and quantitative differences with our previous findings. The average resident (note again, the bedridden, acutely ill, and highly confused were excluded) in both settings is a fairly independent person. Nevertheless, the ratio between dependent and independent self-care behaviors is 1:15 in the nursing home and 1:6 in the home for the chronically ill. It must be noted, however, that the observed frequency of dependent self-care behaviors reported for the nursing home is most likely an underestimation. In contrast to the U.S. homes (with a ratio of 1:4), observations of self-care situations in the West Berlin homes were more restricted by staff, as well as by residents' requests for privacy.

We also find the average resident in both homes to be rather active and constructively engaged (42% in both homes). Nonengaged and sleeping behaviors, however, are as expected more frequent in the home for the chronically ill (ca. 20% of all behaviors) than in the nursing home (ca. 6%).

Looking at the behavior profile of social partners, we continue to observe independence-supportive behaviors to be less frequent than dependence-supportive behaviors. Comparing the two homes, we find fewer independence-supportive and dependence-supportive behaviors, and more engagement-supportive behaviors from social partners in the nursing home than in the home for the chronically ill.

The newly added specification of the dyadic form for each type of behavior allows for some broader understanding of the behaviors observed. Excluding the category miscellaneous other – which due to the narrow definition of the form categories was coded most frequently – we find that the behaviors of residents are most often exhibited as compliance followed by conversation, whereas behaviors of social partners can be characterized most often as conversation followed by suggestion/request/command. Specifically, evidence was obtained that dependent self-care behaviors of residents are mostly exhibited as compliance/cooperation, whereas the complementary behaviors of social partners (dependence-supportive behavior) that follow are in the form of suggestion/request/command. This characterization has the social partners take the directive and initiating part in these interactions, whereas the residents follow suit. That is, the locus of control is in the social environment of the elderly resident, namely the social partners. The very small number of dependent self-care behaviors in the form of suggestion/request/command – reflecting more active help-seeking behaviors – are typically followed by dependence-supportive behavior of social partners in the form of compliance. However, such interactional events, suggestive of a locus of initiation in the elderly, are very rare.

Thus, the notion of passivity of residents is greatly enhanced by this additional coding. Our assumption that dependent self-care of residents might be expressed in active help-seeking behaviors was generally not supported. It is interesting, however, that there was more dependent self-care behavior of residents, as well as dependence-supportive behavior of social partners in the form of suggestion/request/command, in the home for the chronically ill than in the nursing home. Furthermore, behaviors of residents and social partners in the form of refusal, conversation, and cooperation are more frequent in the nursing home than in the home for the chronically ill. The only exception are dependence-related behaviors in the form of cooperation. These are more frequent in the home for the chronically ill.

In general we find, as expected and in accordance with the mortality data of the two samples, more dependency-related behaviors in the home for the chronically ill and more independence-related behaviors in the nursing home.

When looking at the interaction patterns between elderly residents and their social partners, we see that the extension features of coding form and continuity of behavior and including a different setting, the home for the chronically ill, did not alter the basic interaction patterns found in our previous studies. Despite some significant quantitative differences in the behaviors between the two settings, there are similar interaction patterns found in the nursing home and in the home for the chronically ill. In both settings, we find social ecologies that differentiate between dependent and independent behaviors of elderly residents; whereas dependent self-care behavior is most likely followed by support from social partners, independent self-care activities go basically unnoticed by the social ecology. Similarly, nonengaged behaviors and sleeping are typically ignored by social partners. The only positive or self-enhancing behaviors that receive intermittent support from the social environment are behaviors of engagement. The robustness of the patterns is, indeed, substantial. We believe that they can now be regarded as a firmly established empirical fact (see also Dzaman, 1983; Mikulic, 1971). We have also discovered an additional contingency in the nursing-home setting, which occurs when dependent self-care behavior of residents is followed by independent self-care behavior of residents. This is an interesting pattern and needs to be checked out in the next studies. It is interesting because it seems to suggest that residents will perform the task at hand if after waiting or asking for help, no help is forthcoming.

At first glance, our results concerning frequency and contingency seem to be at odds with behavioral principles. I alluded to this before on pages 56 and 93. On the basis of the contingencies observed, one would expect dependent self-care behaviors of the elderly to show the highest frequency, independent self-care as well as nonengaged behaviors to show the lowest frequencies, and constructively engaged behaviors to range in between.

However, careful consideration suggests that these expectations are rather naive. First, as to independent self-care behaviors, it is common in the operant literature (e.g., Patterson, 1982) to find that acquisition and maintenance of behaviors can be, and most often are, governed by different contingencies. The additional differentiation between new (or discontinuous) and old (or continuous) behaviors illuminated the conditions under which independent self-care behaviors of residents can be maintained. The reason to include this coding measure was to determine more closely those behaviors that tend to follow themselves, that is, that tend to lack external social consequences. In the case of independent self-care behavior, the present data show that independent self-care behaviors are significantly more often followed by new behaviors within the same response class. Thus, the lack of social contingencies cannot be excused by the fact that independent self-care behaviors take a long time to be accomplished. The argument that independence-supportive behaviors would be exhibited most likely after the entire task had been achieved and, therefore, would be less frequent after each act of independent self-care, should be dismissed. It is obvious from our data that independent behaviors occur in a progression in strings of different singular acts, which means that they are maintained most likely by chaining. They have become automatic behaviors – habits or mindless behaviors, according to Langer (1983) – and thus do not normally require external reinforcers for their maintenance.

On the other hand, the exhibition of dependent self-care acts is limited by natural circumstances, despite being followed by external social reinforcers. There is a ceiling effect due to the naturally existing occasions in which dependent self-care acts can occur. Furthermore, we should not overlook that our coding system could be biased positively toward independent self-care acts.

Thus, the interaction pattern reflects, at least as far as the domain of self-care is concerned, the microecology of an institutional system characterized by overcare. Ransen (1978) argued that we are dealing with a system in which "residents' needs are routinely overestimated and in which caretaking is overly sufficient to meet actual needs" (p. 61).

What about possible implications for clinical practice in nursing homes and other long-term care institutions? Proceeding from the assumption that it is desirable to care but also to enhance and optimize functioning, we offer the following conclusion (see Baltes, 1987, 1988). The question worthy of discussion in this context is not so much How can we change dependent self-care behaviors? as How can we change the environment so that the instrumental character or function of dependent self-care behavior, namely, securing social contact, is taken over by a different, socially acceptable behavior of the elderly? How can we get staff or social partners to provide social contact in a continuous and immediate fashion following behavior other than dependent self-care? The implications of such change would possibly generate a behavioral and social world in homes for the elderly where phenotypic passivity is not the acceptable norm. On the contrary, such institutions should be able to foster independent care and behavior, rather than discourage it. We will follow up on these questions in Study 14 in Chapter 7.

Summary of Findings with Institutionalized Elderly

All five studies (Studies 3–7) demonstrated two basic interaction patterns: When comparing the social consequences of dependent versus independent self-care behaviors of elderly persons in long-term care institutions, we found that dependent self-care behaviors are typically followed by social actions, and independent self-care behaviors are not. More specifically, the only significant complementary relationship between elderly residents and social partners is dependent self-care behavior followed by dependence-supportive behavior. As to independent self-care, the dominant response of social partners is no response; although this may be adequate according to adult social norms, it does not generate a social interaction sequence. Consequently, dependent behaviors in the context of self-care have the highest probability of being followed continuously and immediately by supportive acts from social partners. While the objective of the institutions in which the data were obtained was to "correct" dependency or at least to "maintain" independence as long as possible, in fact the behavior of the staff tended to reward dependent behavior. We found a consistent pattern, a social script so to speak, in which dependent behavior was supported and considered appropriate. Any weaknesses of the elderly, whether real or expected, were compensated for by the social partners (see Figure 20). As a result, we have labeled these two patterns the "dependency–support script" and the "independence–ignore script."

There are other independent behaviors of the elderly resident, for instance constructively engaged behaviors such as writing a letter or playing a game with a fellow resident, which are followed by supportive consequences from social partners. Yet, compared

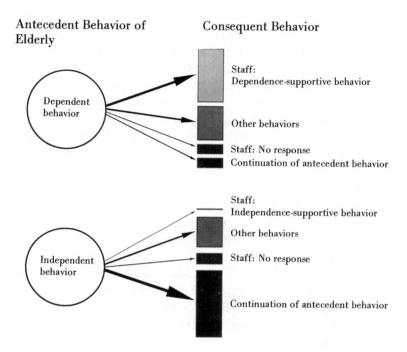

Figure 20. Dependency–support script and independence–ignore script.

to dependent self-care behaviors, such supportive behaviors are exhibited in an inconsistent and irregular manner. This type of response pattern can be interpreted as an intermittent reinforcement schedule. Although this schedule is recognized as a "strong" vehicle for the maintenance of behavior, in the environment of the institution it is a schedule that fails to attract social contact in a reliable and immediate manner. Finally, it should be mentioned that the second category of dependent behaviors, namely nonengaged behaviors, which are the object of frequent complaints by staff, seem to go unnoticed much as independent self-care behaviors do.

Thus, the least amount of social connectedness is associated with passive or nonengaged and independent self-care behaviors. The highest degree of social connectedness is affiliated with dependent self-care behavior, and the second highest with independent constructively engaged behavior. For the elderly, dependent self-care behavior seems to have the highest probability of securing immediate and reliable support, attention, or actions from social partners. Moreover, the dependent self-care situation represents the only truly reciprocal situation in the world of the institutionalized elderly. The meaning for the elderly resident is clear: If I want to have social contact, and continued contact, I must act in a dependent manner.

These results are underscored by the findings about the "dyadic form" of the interaction patterns between residents and social partners. Remember, the reason for introducing codes for dyadic form was to identify more precisely the directionality of the interaction. Most of the behaviors of the elderly are expressed in the form of compliance or cooperation. In contrast, most of the behaviors of social partners take the form of a request/suggestion/command or cooperation. Rarely did we observe refusal or request as an act of the elderly. This additional information seems to support the notion of dominance and directionality running from the social partner to the elderly resident and not vice versa. The elderly seem to comply with what is requested or selected for by the social environment, whether requested directly by the social partner or indirectly by rules of the institution. There are few interactions in which acts on the part of the resident are aimed at producing a change in the social partner's behavior.

An argument has been made that independent behaviors are intrinsically of longer duration than dependent behaviors and, therefore, do not allow immediate social consequences to occur within the 10-second time interval of our observations. To counter this argument, we attempted to code all behaviors for their continuity or discontinuity. The results show that strings of independent behaviors consist mostly of new, that is discontinuous, behaviors rather than ongoing behaviors. Thus, this "chaining" of strings of independent behaviors is an explanatory principle for its maintenance; the chaining operates in the same manner as reinforcing events from the environment – that is, behaviors of social partners. The finding clearly negates the possibility that because of their longer duration consequences for independent behaviors would not follow within the 10-second time interval.

So far I have reported the analyses to address the question about what behavioral consequences follow certain behavioral acts of the elderly. But a complete analysis of the behavioral system of dependence and independence must also address the question as to what behavioral consequences follow behavioral acts of the social partners. The answer is simple. The behavior of social partners prompts complementary behavior from the elderly residents. Specifically, dependence-supportive behaviors of social partners are typically followed by dependent self-care behaviors of residents, independence-supportive behaviors by independent self-care behaviors, engagement-supportive behaviors by constructively engaged behaviors of residents, and so on. We can deduce that the elderly discriminate very well between the different behaviors of social partners and react "appropriately." Since the behavior sequences initiated by social partners and responded to by residents are more complementary than the behavior sequences running from residents to social partners, the directionality of the interaction pattern is one-sided and seems to be determined by the social partner and not by the resident.

An important question has been asked as to interindividual differences in the dependency–support script. Do, for instance, factors such as care status, length of institutionalization, gender, and so on change the dependency–support script? In response, we did look at length of institutionalization, age within this old-age group, and gender and found no effect of these variables on the dependency–support script. We also looked at frequency of dependent and independent behaviors and compared interaction patterns of those people that show the highest scores on dependency and those that show the highest score of independence (Baltes, 1979). Again the patterns are the same.

Conclusions from Observational Findings in Institutions

In view of the patterns identified, I contend that the social world in long-term care institutions is highly structured and differentiated. There is evidence for differential contingencies for the behaviors exhibited by the elderly. Specifically, dependent behaviors lead to dependence-supportive behaviors, independent behaviors to no response. In a recent series of discussions (Baltes & Skinner, 1983; Peterson & Raps, 1984; Raps, Peterson, Jonas, & Seligman, 1982) the question was raised about whether or not institutional settings produce learned helplessness. In line with the present findings, Baltes and Skinner (1983) argued that, in order for dependent or passive behavior to be labeled "helpless" behavior, one would have to demonstrate "noncontingency" in the institution. In other words, behaviors of the elderly would not be followed by differential consequences. If, however, behavior consistently and differentially produces specific consequences, dependent behavior is not the product of learned helplessness but of overcare. I have labeled this model "learned dependency."

The institutional environment, thus, is not one in which helplessness prevails, but a world in which specific behaviors generate specific consequences. It is the dependent rather than the independent behaviors, however, that are instrumental in securing social consequences, such as social contact. The existence of social contingencies for dependent self-care behaviors raises serious doubts about the link between dependency and lack of control or the condition of noncontingency. The present findings thus support not only a differentiation between dependent and independent behaviors but also a differentiation between dependency and lack of control, and consequently, perhaps a differentiation between dependency and the negative effects predicted by the learned-helplessness model.

Two major questions need to be addressed, however. We need to know, on the one hand, whether the observed temporal sequences have functional significance and, on the other hand, whether these interaction patterns are mainly an institutional or an age effect.

Now let us look at the questions concerning generalization across ecologies (institution vs. community) and age (children vs. old people) and possible reasons for the dominance of the dependency–support script in the social world of the elderly.

6

Generalization of Interaction Patterns

RESEARCH QUESTION 2a: *Is the Dependency–Support Script an Institution Effect?*

Comparative Data from Elderly in Community Settings: Qualification of the Dominance of the Dependency–Support Script

We have seen that the basic finding of distinctly different inter-action patterns related to independent and dependent functioning in institutions between elderly residents and their social environ-ment is quite robust. Factors such as length of institutionalization, care status, sex of the resident, type of institution, and age within the old-age group do influence the frequency of behaviors, but the basic patterns of the observed behavior sequences are changed only slightly. Thus, within and across institutions the patterns seemed consistent.

But what about the generalizability of the findings to other ecologies such as the general community? The best way to address this issue of *setting specificity* would be via a longitudinal study of old people before and after institutionalization. In a first ap-proach to this question, I can offer comparative cross-sectional data with elderly who dwell in the community.

STUDY 8 (Baltes & Wahl, 1992; Wahl & Baltes, 1990)

Given research findings suggesting reduced competence in the in-stitutionalized elderly (for review see Baltes, Wahl, & Reichert, 1991), we venture, as our first hypothesis, to show a behavioral profile in the community setting that contains relatively more independence-related behaviors. In line with this thinking and the related trend toward promoting home care and preventing institutionalization, we also predict interactional patterns in the community setting that reflect more social reactions (such as independence-supportive behaviors) following independent behaviors. Thus, our second hypothesis foresees a weakening of the pervasiveness of the dependency–support script observed in institutions in favor of a social interaction pattern in the community setting that also includes attention to independent behaviors.

Samples and Setting. To recruit participants, we advertised in newspapers and on radio programs, as well as in the community health-care offices. In two separate efforts a total of 22 elderly people ($N = 13$ being visited in the mornings by home health nurses; $N = 9$ interacting with family members) participated (Baltes & Wahl, 1992; Wahl & Baltes, 1990). All elderly participants received some assistance during morning care either from family members or from home health nurses, but all were oriented to person, time, and place. Whether they were receiving family or nurse's assistance, elderly participants did not differ with regard to gender, age, mobility, or functional health. They varied, although not systematically, with regard to socioeconomic status and education. The average age was about 79.5 years, ranging between 70 and 90 years. Looking at the mortality data of institutionalized elderly (Study 7) and elderly in the community (Study 8), we found that mortality rates were significantly higher in the home for the chronically ill than in the nursing home group and somewhat higher, but not significantly so, in the two community groups than in the nursing home group.[4]

As to the social world of the elderly participants, all staff members, home health nurses, and family members who were interacting with the elderly participants were observed as social partners. Specifically, there were 8 staff members interacting with the nursing home group and 15 with the chronically ill group. For the community group, 9 home health nurses – 4 of whom were observed in interaction with more than one of the elderly participants – were observed, along with 9 family members, usually spouses or adult children.

With regard to the settings, community dwelling participants lived in the western part of Berlin and varied with regard to type of housing (apartment vs. house) and type of neighborhood. They lived alone, with a spouse, with children, or with other relatives. The settings for the institutionalized elderly have been described in the previous study 7 (Baltes et al., 1987).

Design and Procedure. The same observational coding scheme developed for institutions was applied. In addition, we also coded the kind of self-care activity the elderly performed and differentiated among basic personal care, ambulating, eating, and housework.[5]

Observer Training and Agreement. The training of observers was identical to that described for the studies in institutions (see page 50). The procedure for collecting reliability data, however, had to be different. For practical and ethical reasons, interobserver agreement in the traditional sense (i.e., comparison by two observers observing at the same time in the same place) could not be secured in the community setting. Instead, agreement with a *standard,* as well as agreement on the part of each observer over time (within-observer *stability*) were used as reliability measures. First, the coding performance of each observer was checked weekly via videotaped scenes and compared to a standard. The standard represents the codings of these scenes by the author. Using Cohen's kappa statistic (Cohen, 1960; Hollenbeck, 1978), perfect agreement ($K = 1$) was defined so that the observer had to code exactly the same events (type, form, continuity code, etc.) in the same sequence over time as those listed in the standard coding. The mean kappa averaged over all sessions amounted to .73 (SD = .11).

Second, within-observer stability was based on examination of randomly selected observation sessions recorded by the same observer observing the same person at two different times (in general, at a 4-week interval). It was assumed that the interactions between the focus person and his or her partner would not change much over such short time periods. Perfect agreement was defined as a point-by-point agreement between two protocols by the same observer observing the same dyad. Mean kappa was .80 (SD = .12). In this instance, the observers did not know which sessions would be used for stability assessment.

Observational Procedure, Observational Session, Observational Unit, and Total Observation Time. In contrast to the institutional setting, in the community setting the only consistent and regular time of interaction between the target elderly and their partners occurred during the morning. Each morning session lasted, on average, 50.4 minutes in the home health care group (HH) and 54.7 minutes in the family care group (FC). Each participant was observed on average 12.7 days (HH) and 11.7 days (FC). Thus, on average community participants were observed a total of 10 hours distributed across at least 7 days. The data collection in the community setting took about 9 months.

Identical to the institutional studies, the behavioral stream between focus person and partner was observed continuously in 10-second time samples for the entire session (3 minutes in the institutions; about 50 minutes in the community dwellings). Thus, the observational unit of 10 seconds for the behaviors of focus person and partner was the same across settings and actors. When the partner left the room, this was coded and the behavior coding of the focus person continued. In addition, the event of observation (morning self-care) was identical in all four groups and in all groups there was only one observer present. (The reliability data gathered in the institutions did not enter into the data matrix.) Furthermore, the number of observational sessions per focus person hardly differed (average of 12.2 sessions in the community setting versus about 13 sessions in the institutional setting).

Thus, the only difference between the two settings was the total time that each subject was observed. In terms of total time per session, this is a difference between 3 minutes versus about 50 minutes per focus person. It should be noted that this over-sampling of time observed in the community setting was planned to offset the small sample size of the community groups ($N = 13$ and $N = 9$) compared to the institutional groups ($N = 39$ each). An extended observation time per subject would, we hoped, compensate for a potential lack in representativeness of the observational data resulting from the smaller number of subjects in the community groups. Nevertheless, this difference in total time of observation is reflected in the larger number of events observed in the morning session for the two community groups. Thus, differences in behavioral frequencies between the groups are a confound of setting, person, and total time of observation. Therefore, only behavioral profiles or relative frequencies between groups can and will be compared.

Findings. Remember, the present study was undertaken to gain information about the generalizability of the *dependency–support script,* the dominant interaction pattern observed in the institutional setting. In addition, we explored whether the social response pattern following independent self-care may be pronounced in the community setting. In the institutional setting independent behavior was largely ignored. The following is a summary of the findings reporting first on the behavior profiles and then on the interaction patterns.

It should come as no surprise that there are similarities and differences with the institutional findings. The major difference points to more self-care-related behaviors in the community than in the institutional setting. In the two institutional groups the relative frequency of self-care behaviors of the elderly account for about 50% and 30%; in the community groups for about 77% and 74%. Social partners in the settings also display a different relative frequency. In the institutional groups about 36% and 57% are care-related, in the community groups the figures are about 75% in both groups. That the morning was the primary context in which care was offered to the elderly participants in the community setting is one explanation for this difference. With regard to other interactions dispersed throughout the day, we assume that they were rare in the community setting. We do not have, however, systematic information about the remainder of the day. We only know from an interdisciplinary study, the Berlin Aging study, that elderly spend the majority of their day alone (Baltes et al., 1993).

Turning to the interaction patterns, there are similarities as well as differences between the institutional and community setting (see Figure 21). The similarity concerns the social contingencies following dependent self-care behavior, the dissimilarity concerns

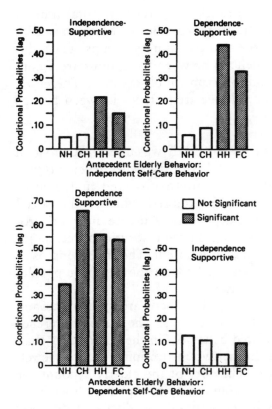

Figure 21. Lag results for two behaviors of community elderly and their social partners (HH and FC) compared to those of nursing home elderly (NH) and the home of chronically ill (CH).

the contingencies that follow independent self-care behavior. In both settings, dependent self-care behavior was followed significantly by dependence-supportive behavior on the part of social partners, thus affirming the dependency–support script as a clearly recognizable interaction pattern in both settings. Note, however, that dependent behavior not only secures immediate and reliable reactions (dependence-supportive behaviors), but this reliable and powerful connection also identifies dependent self-care behaviors as an instrument with which the elderly can control certain environmental events. The dependence-supportive behaviors are complementary responses by the social partner and thus reinforcing.

The dissimilarity between the institutional and community ecology is strongest for the case of independent self-care (see Figure 21). In the institutional setting, this antecedent behavior (aside from being less frequent) is largely ignored by social partners. In only one nursing home did we find some significance for independence-supportive behavior of staff following independent behavior of residents. Independent behaviors seem to occur in a vacuum. In the community setting, independent self-care behavior is followed by a highly ambivalent social pattern. It is followed about 28% of the time by social responses. These consequent events to independent self-care behaviors of the elderly are twice as often supportive of dependence rather than independence.

Conclusions about Generalization across Setting

What are the implications of the dominance of the dependency–support script and the ambivalent contingencies for independence? First, an orientation toward dependency in both settings indicates that the perception of older people as incompetent dominates the social partners' interactional patterns. This line of argument is strengthened by the present data, which demonstrate the existence of a noncomplementary or extinction schedule associated with independent behavior in the community groups. Although in the community setting there is a recognition of independent self-care, this recognition is marked by a prevalence of mismatched social responses. The assumption that this social script may reflect expectations of incompetence by social partners is also supported by observational research involving children (see pages 118–126). In children, other clusters of independent behaviors (e.g., constructively engaged behaviors) evoke complementary responses and social connectedness. Thus, age seems to be a main force in the interactional dynamics, which is further underlined by the institutional setting.

Finally, what about the ambivalence toward independent self-care in the community setting? Reconstructing the temporal sequences involving independent behaviors of the elderly along operant learning principles, one can argue that both an extinction schedule (independent behavior followed by dependence-supportive behavior) and a reinforcement schedule (independent behavior followed by independence-supportive behavior) coexist in the community setting. On the one hand, we need to note that the sheer existence of a social response to independent self-care is important. On the other hand, the occurrence of twice as many incongruent (dependence-supportive) as congruent (independence-supportive) social responses can be expected to have negative effects on the elderly's disposition to continue to show independent self-care. Applying a social learning perspective, one would expect independent behaviors to decline over time. Such an interpretation, however, needs longitudinal examination, an endeavor that is very difficult to realize. Initially we had hoped to extend our community study into a longitudinal one, but we were deterred by lack of funding.

RESEARCH QUESTION 2b: *Is the Dependency–Support Script an Age-Specific Effect?*

Comparative Studies with Children: Development-Enhancing Interaction Patterns

A second avenue to discriminate between setting effect and age effect was to study children and their social partners.

STUDY 9 (Baltes, Reisenzein, & Kindermann, 1985)

When considering institutions for children our goal was to look for a type of institution that would most closely approximate institutions for the elderly. We decided on homes for orphans and neglected children. To minimize the potential uniqueness of a particular institution and to secure a larger pool of potential subjects, two very different homes caring for orphans and neglected children were selected.

Description of Institutional Settings. Home A and B differ in their proprietorship (A is state-owned, B has a religious affiliation), their location (A is located in the northern suburbs of [former] West Berlin, B in the more central part of the city), and in the physical appearance of the buildings (B is a renovated but old building, A is relatively new and modern). Both homes were organized in groups consisting of 7 to 10 children of different ages together with 3 to 4 staff members. Each group lived on separate floors of the home and formed an independent unit as far as daily living was concerned. At the time of observation, the staff members of Home B happened to be exclusively females.

Participants. Observations were made of three groups of Home A and of one group of Home B. The sample of the target children totaled 15 in Home A and 5 in Home B. Mean age of the Home A sample was 12.25 years (SD = 1.29) and 8.8 years (SD = 2.33) in the Home B sample. Mean length of institutionalization of the Home A sample was 1.46 years (SD = 1.43) and 3.27 years (SD = 2.35) in the Home B sample.

Social partners comprised staff and other children in the groups. Both children and staff members were individually approached for informed consent in order to participate.

Observer training, agreement procedures, and observational procedures were identical to those used in the institutions for elderly.

Findings. We reasoned that if the interaction patterns between children and their social partners were similar to those observed for elderly residents and their social partners, this would be an indication that the institution per se, regardless of the age of its inhabitants, is responsible for the observed interaction patterns.

The essential differences between the age groups (children vs. elderly) can be summarized as follows. First, dependent self-care behavior, the main instrumental act of the elderly to gain social reactions and contact, loses its dominance in the case of children. Constructively engaged behaviors take over this function, which is represented both in the behavioral frequencies (see Figure 22) and the interaction patterns (see Figure 23).

Second, the interaction patterns between children and their social partners evince greater bidirectionality or reciprocity when compared with the interaction patterns between elderly and their social partners. All behaviors of the target children (e.g., construc-

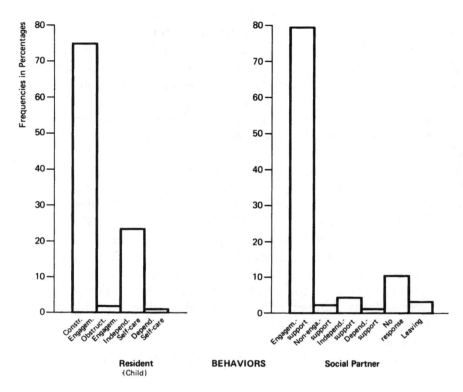

Figure 22. Behavioral frequencies for children and their social partners.

tively engaged, dependent, and independent self-care behaviors) were followed very consistently by the respective *complementary* behaviors of their social partners and vice versa. Hence, it can be said that both the children's behaviors and those of their social partners exert similar discriminative control with regard to the behaviors of their partners.

In contrast, for elderly residents reciprocity was found to be true only with regard to dependent behaviors. The behavior of the elderly seems, therefore, to be less conducive to complementary responses than the behavior of institutionalized children. There is far more behavioral reciprocity in the homes for children than in the homes for the elderly, and children's behavior patterns seem to be directed more toward behaviors that enhance their development – that is, their autonomy, growth, and optimization.

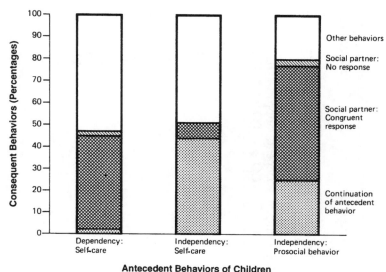

Figure 23. Interaction patterns for institutionalized children and their social partners.

This is also portrayed in the dyadic form of the behaviors of staff and children. In contrast to the findings with the institutionalized elderly, both children and their social partners show more frequent cooperation and compliance.

This notion of unidirectionality is underscored further when considering both the "control" and "power" indexes of the contingencies (Patterson, 1982). Patterson (1982) uses the term *power* in addition to *control* (as defined by the presence of contingency) to explain the variance of the contingency accounted for by the antecedent event. Looking at Table 13 we can see that in the case of the elderly, the most significant control and power is exerted by dependent self-care behavior (Baltes & Reisenzein, 1986). This means that dependent behaviors are typically followed by dependence-supportive behaviors, and dependence-supportive behaviors are typically preceded by dependent behaviors. Constructively engaged behaviors of the elderly exhibit more power than control; although engaged behaviors of the elderly typically precede engagement-supportive behaviors of social partners, they often occur without being followed by engagement-

Table 13. Control and Power Indexes for Each Behavior of Institutionalized Residents and Children as Antecedents and Behaviors of the Social Partners as Consequents Separately for Each Group

Antecedent Events		Consequent Events						Base Probability
		Engag.-Supp.		Indep.-Supp.		Depend.-Supp.		
		CO	PO	CO	PO	CO	PO	
Constructively engaged	U.S.	.20	.75					.23
	E1	.28	.88					.52
	E2	.14	.84					.52
	Ch	.51	.91					.69
Obstructively engaged	U.S.				.17			.03
	E1	.23			.17			.02
	E2	.16						.01
	Ch	.62						.01
Nonengaged	U.S.							.52
	E1							.16
	E2							.11
	Ch							.02

Independent self-care							
U.S.				.34			.19
E1			.05	.76			.28
E2				.45			.30
Ch			.07	.57		.58	.28
Dependent self-care							
U.S.	.10	.05	.05	.26	.47	.57	.03
E1			.07	.07	.44	.39	.02
E2			.11	.24	.56	.57	.06
Ch			.08		.19	.17	.01

Note: CO = control; PO = power. Conditional probabilities with $p < .05$ and $N > 20$ and with a positive deviation only are shown in the table. U.S. refers to nursing home residents in central Pennsylvania; E1 and E2 represent nursing home residents in Berlin, FRG; Ch refers to a group of institutionalized children in Berlin, FRG.

supportive behaviors from social partners. In the case of the institutionalized children, in contrast, it is constructively engaged behavior that possesses the most significant power and control. In addition, obstructively engaged behaviors show significant control but little power and conversely, independent self-care behaviors have significant power but little control.

Thus, the contingency pattern of dependent self-care behaviors followed by dependence-supportive behaviors, which has been identified as being the most likely pattern in long-term care institutions for the elderly, is also present in the children's homes, but it is infrequent and is largely due to dependent self-care behaviors displayed as requests, suggestions, or commands, which are typically followed by dependence-supportive behaviors in the form of compliance.

The third and final essential difference, extending from this finding about the form of dependent behavior, refers to the impression that dependence-supportive behaviors follow mainly dependent self-care behaviors that are due to true *incompetence* of the child. This interpretation is corroborated by the findings from Kindermann (1993).

STUDY 10 (Kindermann, 1993)

Kindermann used the same observational procedure except that we decided on employing videocameras to record the interaction patterns between toddlers and their mothers occurring in their own homes during routine activities related to eating, dressing, and walking. The patterns demonstrate that schedules of reinforcement for dependent or independent behaviors are tailor-made to fit the level of competence of the toddler. When the child is ready to master a new domain – for instance, to eat independently – the mother most likely exhibits independence-supportive behavior. In contrast, when the child has not yet reached this developmental stage, the child's dependent behaviors – for the domain of eating – are met with dependence-supportive behaviors of the mother. During the learning stage, the same dependent behaviors are met with independence-supportive behaviors; once the child has mastered the task, the mother most likely ignores that independent behavior of the child (Kindermann, 1993).

The dependency–support script dominating the ecology of the

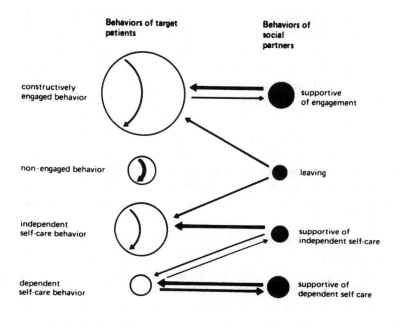

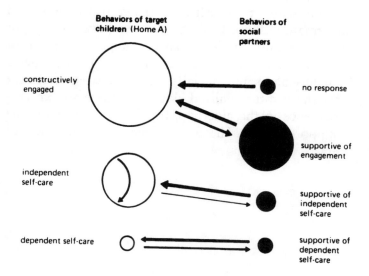

Figure 24. Summary of interaction patterns for elderly in the home for chronically ill and children in Home A.

elderly seems to suggest, therefore, that the elderly are perceived of as incompetent or prone to dependency. This perception by social partners is not necessarily a valid one. As shown by operant-experimental findings on dependent behaviors of the elderly (see pages 36–40; for reviews see Baltes & Barton, 1979; Hussian, 1981; Mosher-Ashley, 1986–1987), the elderly are quite often capable of performing the required behaviors, and their dependent behaviors can be reversed by appropriate management of environmental contingencies. Immediate help or assistance that is offered by social partners regardless of whether the elderly needs or wants it may foster dependent behavior. Figure 24 summarizes the large differences in the interaction patterns between elderly and children.

The comparative data support the interpretation of the interaction patterns between the elderly and their social partners as being mainly an age-related rather than an institution-related phenomenon. The findings suggest that there is greater reciprocity and balance in the social world of children. Institutionalized children and their social partners interact on more even terms when it comes to codetermining their interactions. This age-related interpretation is strengthened further by the findings on natural interactions in the context of self-care between toddlers and mothers (Kindermann, 1993). Children seem to have more input in determining the nature of the social exchange, and more of their behavioral repertoire is responded to in a fashion conducive to a development-enhancing, socially supportive environment than is true for the institutionalized elderly. Is there an expectation of incompetence in the elderly which is the reason for the dependency–support script? The next studies were designed to give us answers.

7

Expectations and Attributions

RESEARCH QUESTION 3: *What Explains the Behavior of Social Partners?*

What Understanding Do People Have of Concepts Like Independence and Dependence?

We have argued (see for instance, Baltes, Wahl, & Reichert, 1991) that the exclusiveness of the dependency–support script implies approval of dependent behaviors as adequate behaviors on the part of staff members. One major factor in the production of the dependency–support script is very likely professional and social expectations about old persons. Expecting elderly residents to be prone to dependency would be in line with the staff's professional socialization and understanding of their helping role (Karuza, Rabinowitz, & Zevon, 1986) as well as with the staff's negative attitudes toward aging, which are frequently reported in the literature (for review see Baltes, Wahl, & Reichert, 1991). The pervasiveness of the dependency–support script is not surprising and surely not a new idea if we consider the long-standing discussion on autonomy and loss of autonomy in institutions (Collopy, 1990; Goffman, 1961; Hofland, 1990).

STUDY 11 (Reichert, 1993)

Quasi-Experimental Study: Expectation of Incompetence. In order to test the validity of our interpretation, Reichert (1993), in a quasi-experimental design, attempted to test the effect of expectations of social partners on their helping (dependence-supportive) behavior. For the manipulation of professional expectation, she compared nurses and educators who were asked to interact with elderly people in problem-solving situations. Both situation (nursing home vs. scientific institute) and competence level of the elderly were systematically varied. The variation in situation was to manipulate the negative aging stereotype in that the nursing home is reinforcing the stereotype, the scientific institution is correcting it. All interactions were videotaped and then coded by a blind coder. The interactions between nurses and elderly persons were significantly different from those between educators and elderly, and they were characterized by more direct and immediate helping behaviors. It is tempting to interpret this behavior of nurses as the result of the "medical helping model" (described earlier), in which responsibilities for solutions to problems are taken over by the environment.

STUDY 12 (Wahl, 1991)

Combined Observational and Interview Study: Expectation of Incompetence. An expectation of incompetence is confirmed further by the attributional style held by elderly and their social partners with regard to dependent and independent behaviors. When confronting elderly persons and their partners with their respective observed behaviors, Wahl (1991) found that social partners ascribed responsibility for dependent behaviors to the elderly but attributed independent behavior of the elderly to their own (the social partner's) doing. In contrast, the elderly ascribed independent behavior to themselves, and dependent behavior either to illness or to their environment (i.e., the behavior of social partners).

Wahl (1991), combining the sequential observational design with an interview technique, looked at the relationship between actual behavior and self-efficacy beliefs of the elderly and at attributions of competence or incompetence of the elderly made by themselves and their social partners. The study was conducted with the elderly and their social partners in both institutional and community settings. Nurses were the social partners in the institutional setting, home health nurses in the community setting. For coding the interview data, Wahl developed a method to code information about values and goals concerning independence and dependence, efficacy and self-control, as well as causal explanations for independence and dependence.

From these data we can discern quite diverse attributional styles for the elderly and their social partners. First, as in earlier studies, the elderly who exhibit dependent behaviors are supported for these behaviors. Second – a new finding – self-efficacy beliefs influence independent behavior in that elderly with higher self-efficacy beliefs show more independent behaviors. Third, the elderly credited themselves for independent behavior and attributed dependent behavior to staff's behavior or to their own impairments. In contrast, staff credited themselves for the independent behavior of the elderly, and thought that dependent behavior was caused by the residents (e.g., they claimed the residents refused to act, were lazy, did not listen to instructions, etc.).

STUDY 13 (Schmid-Furstoss, 1990)

Interview Study: Laypersons' Conceptions of Dependency and Independence. Schmid-Furstoss (1990) analyzed older people's subjective or naive theories about independence and dependence from three different settings: community dwellings, senior apartment housing, and a nursing home.

When asked to give a definition of the concept of dependency and to describe causes and consequences of dependency, community-living elderly as well as seniors in apartment housing defined dependency as mental incompetence whereas nursing home residents more frequently labeled it as physical incompetence.

Likewise, nursing home residents gave physical impairments as the major cause of dependency, whereas the other two groups attributed dependency to environmental factors and to loss in decision making and control. All three groups thought there were negative emotional consequences of dependency; in addition senior apartment residents and community-living elderly added helplessness and passivity as frequent consequences of dependency.

Summary of Data on Subjective Perceptions of Dependency and Independence

The dependency–support script is a reality for the elderly and their social partners. The two groups have, however, quite distinct notions about who is responsible for dependency and its social support. Each blames the other. The elderly believe it is the environment that limits their action and makes them dependent, and that declining health is a contributing factor. Their social partners, in contrast, believe it is the elderly's lack of effort that is responsible for dependency. In the case of independence, both parties want to take responsibility. The social partners believe they stimulate the elderly to be independent; the elderly believe it is their own effort and will that cause independent behaviors. Changing the behavior of the social partner, then, may be the best way to rewrite the dependency–support script or better to introduce an independence–support script in the social world of the elderly. Thus, we come to our last research question concerning the modifiability of the interaction patterns.

Ecological Intervention Research: Optimization of Environmental Conditions in Institutions

RESEARCH QUESTION 4: *Can We Change the Dependency–Support Script?*

Given increasing numbers of the very old, institutions will remain important living environments in the proximate future, even if community-based care is markedly expanded. Thus, designing institutions in ways that facilitate independence despite frailty becomes an increasingly important objective, particularly in light of the linkage between autonomy and well-being (Baltes, Wahl, Reichert, 1991; Baltes, 1995).

As you have seen so far, we have been able to identify a behavioral system that exists in the ecology of the elderly that might be responsible for dependent behavior. The central theme of this research focused on social environmental conditions involved in fostering dependent behavior. To identify the contextual conditions of dependency, a methodology of sequential observations was used to record the behavioral stream between elderly people and their social partners in the natural environment. Findings of our sequential observational studies demonstrated two reliable and robust interaction patterns: the dependency–support script and the independence–ignore script. These scripts signify that dependent behavior, of all behavior of the elderly, is the most likely to result in social contact and attention. Accordingly, behavioral dependency is instrumental for the elderly in controlling the environment, specifically social contact with staff – a highly valued commodity in institutions.

We have argued before (Baltes & Wahl, 1991) that the dependency–support script, applied across people without consideration of their different competence levels, may reflect overcare. The high prevalence of this pattern suggests that it is a social script, meaning that staff members accept the script as role-congruent and appropriate for the competence level of the elderly (see also Wahl, 1991; Reichert, 1993). Such a behavioral script anticipates real or expected weaknesses of the residents. In the case of real weaknesses or incompetence, this is an appropriate and humane interaction pattern. In contrast, when weaknesses are merely expected, the supportive behavior of staff may induce behavioral dependency. Accordingly, the dependency–support script may, in the long run, foster decline because the elderly are not using and practicing skills they still possess.

These findings point to the desirability of interventions geared toward changing environmental conditions to offer as much autonomy as possible within a prosthetic setting. Can we change the behavior of social partners such that more attention and emphasis is given to independent behaviors of the elderly? Can we create an independence–support script to replace or compensate for the dependency–support script whenever there is an instance of overcare?

STUDY 14 (Baltes, Neumann, & Zank, 1994)

In order to test the potential for change, we developed a training program for staff aimed at increasing the independence–support and decreasing the dependency–support patterns. The results will support the functional validity of temporal interaction patterns and point to practical implications such as training caregivers to be more aware of the importance of balance between dependency and autonomy for the elderly (Parmelee & Lawton, 1990).

To examine the feasibility and utility of the training program, an intervention study was designed to analyze three hypotheses:

1. Staff members who participate in the training program will show an increase in behavior that promotes independence.
2. Staff members who participate in the training program will show a change in interaction patterns such that the dependency–support script becomes less dominant and the independence–support script is strengthened.
3. Behavior of elderly residents will change as a consequence of an increase in independence-supportive behavior.

Settings. In order to secure greater generalizability of the effects of the training program, three institutions were selected: a state-run nursing home, a religiously affiliated nursing home, and a ward in a geriatric hospital.

The *state-run nursing home* was situated in a lower class district in the southwest of Berlin. The relatively new building had six stories, two of which housed residents who received skilled nursing care. Residents' rooms were two-bed rooms and equipped with furniture typical of a hospital. Almost every resident received social welfare, a rather common situation in Germany. In total, 10 staff members (2 males and 8 females) and 45 residents (4 males and 41 females) were observed. Eight of the staff members had a professional education of some sort.

The *religiously affiliated (Protestant) nursing home* was a three-story building situated in a quiet, middle-class section of the city surrounded by green areas. There were mostly single and a few double rooms, equipped with personal furniture. Twenty-seven residents (3 males, 24 females) took part in the study. Some received social welfare, but most did not. Nine female staff members participated in the study; all had professional education.

The two nursing homes differed markedly in atmosphere and philosophy of care. The religiously affiliated home tried to treat residents as individuals with different needs and wishes. Residents had their own furniture and could choose to have breakfast any time between 8 and 10 a.m. In the state-run home, residents were requested to rise at 6 a.m. and wait for breakfast, set for 8 a.m. There was no difference in need for assistance or frailty of the residents in the two homes.

The *ward in a geriatric hospital* was part of a state-run hospital for chronically ill elderly. It was situated in a lower-middle-class neighborhood. Rooms housed 3 to 8 patients. Thirty-four female patients were observed. Private or governmental health insurances paid for their stay. Eight female staff members participated. All had professional education.

Participants. A total of 27 staff members (8–10 members from each institution) took part in the study, 14 in the experimental and 13 in the control group. Educational and professional background of the staff participants is presented in Table 14. They all worked the morning shift and each staff member was responsible for about the same number of residents per morning, although not always the same residents each morning. Although the official staff-to-resident ratio differed across the three institutions (about 1:4 in the two nursing homes and 1:1.6 in the geriatric ward), in reality these ratios were hardly ever achieved in any one of the homes because of sick days and holidays. For the most part, in all three homes on any morning two staff members were responsible for about 10 to 12 residents.

The residents comprised a total of 106 participants. Their ages ranged from 68 to 91 years with an average age of 83.2 years. Most of them were women (99 women compared to 7 men). All residents received skilled nursing care but were neither completely bedridden nor moderately or severely demented. On average, they suffered from either one or both of two diseases common in old age, namely cardiovascular and skeletal diseases.

Training Program. The training program is activated in two steps. The first step comprises a more theoretical part and is designed to create a knowledge base. The knowledge base taps three domains, which are taught in 10 group sessions (see Table 15).

The three domains are communication, cognitive restructuring, and behavior management.

1. Learning basic communication skills to be used during training but also particularly in working with residents and relating to colleagues.
2. Learning updated facts about aging is intended to explain aspects of behavioral plasticity and modifiability in old age and the role of the environment in aging.

Table 14. *Demographic Characteristics of Staff*

Variables	Experimental Group	Control Group	Total (Same Shift)
N	14	13	27
Gender			
Female	12	13	25
Male	2	0	2
Age			
< 40	9	7	16
> 40	3	4	7
Missing	2	2	4
Marital Status			
Single	7	6	13
Married	2	2	4
Divorced	2	3	5
No information	3	2	5
Education			
Primary school	2	2	4
Training school	5	5	10
High school	4	3	7
Gymnasium		1	1
No information	3	2	5
Professional Training			
Nursing and			
Gerontological nursing	7	10	17
Other	3	1	4
None	2	0	2
No information	2	2	4
Institution			
State-run	6	4	10
Religious	3	5	8
Geriatric ward	5	4	9
Residents			
State-run			45
Religious			34
Geriatric ward			27

3. Learning about behavior management relates to the basic behavioral or learning principles from operant learning psychology. (An extensive step-by-step description of these sessions and their contents is available in Neumann, Zank, Tzschätzsch, and Baltes, 1994.)

In a second step, the *practical application* to everyday nursing care is promoted; it consists of the design, implementation, and evaluation of a behavior modification program. Each participant is given individual assistance in the establishment of the behavior modification program that she conducts with a specific resident (who agreed to and participated in the planning). During the direct and individual supervision staff–resident interactions were videotaped. This part of the program lasted four weeks. Two final evaluative group sessions gave each participant the opportunity to report on his or her behavior modification program and also to express thoughts about the entire training program and further integration into practice.

Design and Procedure. A pre–post control group design was implemented. Pre- and postassessments consisted of daily observations of staff–resident interactions over a 6-week period, collected by trained observers using a coding scheme and an electronic data collection apparatus. Control groups received the same pre- and postassessments but no intervention. The intervention took place in the field during working hours.

Observational Procedure.[6] Pre- and postintervention observations were collected from the same residents and staff members. Observations of the behavior stream between residents and staff began when a staff person entered the room of an elderly resident. The behavioral stream was coded continuously in 10-second observational units for the duration of the entire session, on average 1.5 hours (range 1.0–3.0 hours).

Behavior of staff and residents was coded in a turn-taking fashion. When the behavior of the elderly person continued longer than 10 seconds and the partner did not respond within the 10-second interval, the behavior was recoded. The score–rescore criterion of 10 seconds had been selected empirically. It was long

Table 15. *Training Program*

Theoretical Part	
Session 1:	*Communication Skills* A. Introduction of participants and trainers B. Overview of communication skills (listening, reflecting, speaking) C. Aging Quiz A (modified version of Palmore, 1977, 1981)
Session 2:	*Institutionalization, Institutional Routines, Emotional Support in Institutions* A. Sharing of own work experiences in institutions B. Reasons for and consequences of institutionalization C. Emotional support for residents of institutions
Session 3:	*Etiology of Dependent Behavior in Old Age* A. Impairments B. Helping styles C. Reasons for reinforcement of dependent behavior
Session 4:	*Social Perception of Old Age – Helping Role* A. Reflection of own perceptions of residents B. Effective use of biographical information in interactions with residents C. Reflection of reasons for own job choice
Session 5:	*Stereotypes of Old Age – Biological Deficit Model* A. Discussion of the answers to the Aging Quiz B. Discussion of different models of aging
Session 6:	*Behavior Modification: Rules and Application* A. A successful case of behavior modification B. Basic principles of behavior modification C. Video examples of independence training in elderly residents
Session 7:	*German Nursing Guidelines of Rehabilitation* A. Criteria for quality nursing care B. Organization of nursing care C. Planning of nursing care

Table 15. (*cont.*)

Theoretical Part	
Session 8:	*Transfer of Rehabilitation Guidelines into Praxis* A. Help toward self-help. Illustration with teaching films B. Planning of a sample case of a behavior modification program: A resident is to relearn brushing her teeth C. Role playing of the program among the training participants
Sessions 9 and 10:	*Planning of a Behavior Modification Program* A. Designing a behavior modification program with a resident of own choice B. Group discussions about the designs C. Decision about and concrete documentation of the program
Practical Part	

Implementation of each individual behavior modification program; at minimum five to six concrete practice sessions; three to four video-assisted individual supervision sessions.

Session 11:	*Evaluation of Behavior Modification Program* Each participant shared videos of his/her program. Discussion about experiences and about further possibilities of behavior modification programs with other residents.
Session 12:	*Evaluation of Entire Training Program* Written feedback about training program Aging Quiz B Questionnaire about the taught content.

enough to reflect the natural reaction time on the part of staff and short enough to avoid too many re-recordings of ongoing behaviors of residents. The existence of the score–rescore criterion was critical for statistical analyses in that it provided a standardization of the duration of behaviors across focus persons and social partners.

In the case of simultaneous behaviors exhibited by the focus person or the staff, the rule was to code self-care behaviors first and any other concurrent behavior (like conversation about the weather) second.

When the staff member left the room, this was coded and the behavior coding of the elderly person continued for 1 minute. This 1-minute interval was established to ensure that staff members would not return to the resident. The observer then left the resident, went looking for the staff member, and started coding whenever the staff member began interacting with another resident.

It is important to note that, within each institution, staff members of the experimental and the control groups were observed interacting with the same residents. By observing each staff member with each resident, we avoided systematic biases toward particular staff–resident dyads.

Although great care was taken to have the same number of observational sessions, in this case six, per staff member during the pre- and posttest phase, the total time of observation per staff member varied because of the variation in the time she or he spent with the resident in morning care. There was no systematic variation between staff members in that specific staff members spent more time in morning care each and every day. Nevertheless, this difference in total time of observation is reflected in the differences in the number of events observed for the different staff members. Thus, differences in behavioral frequencies among staff members are a confound of the variables setting, person, and total time of observation. Therefore, only behavioral profiles or relative frequencies between experimental or control group and institutions are compared.

Observer Training and Agreement. Observers were trained with the use of an observation training manual from previous work (see description on page 50) until an observer agreement of .80 (kappa) was reached. Ongoing training during data collection continued weekly.

Videotaping was done by trained student assistants. Each staff member of the experimental group was videotaped three to four times during the pretest and intervention phases when interaction with residents took place.

Findings. A total of 45,092 behavioral events for staff (experimental group: 12,103 in pretest, 10,868 in posttest; control group: 12,058 in pretest, 10,063 in posttest) and 52,416 behavioral events for residents (28,182 in pretest, 24,234 in posttest) were collected. Specifically, there were 8,997 independence-supportive behaviors (experimental group: 2,042 in pretest, 3,014 in posttest; control group: 2,057 in pretest, 1,884 in posttest) and 19,517 dependence-supportive behaviors (experimental group: 5,447 in pretest, 3,938 in posttest; control group: 5,594 in pretest, 4,538 in posttest). For residents there were 8,693 independent behavioral events in pretest, 8,147 in posttest, and there were 11,331 dependent events in pretest, 9,112 in posttest.

To test for differences in the *behavior profiles* presented in Figure 25, two analyses of variance with repeated measures were computed with institution and group as independent factors and time of measurement and behavior category as within group factors. Dependent variables were the percent frequencies of staff behaviors (independence- and dependence-supportive behavior) or the percent frequencies of residents' behaviors (dependent and independent behavior).

Both analyses show, as hypothesized, a significant three-way interaction effect for group (experimental versus control) by time (pre- vs. postintervention) by behavior category (independence- vs. dependence-related behaviors). In the analysis of variance for staff behavior (see Table 16, part I), univariate comparisons reveal that effects are due to both an increase in independence-supportive and a decrease in dependence-supportive behavior.

For the analysis of variance with the behavioral percentages of residents (see Table 16, part II) univariate analyses indicate that the significant effect is due to an increase of independent behavior.

To analyze differences between experimental and control groups from pre- to posttest in the *interaction patterns,* a 3 (Institution) × 2 (Group) × 2 (Time of Measurement) × 4 (Interaction Category) analysis of variance with repeated measures was computed. There were four interaction categories: dependent behavior followed by dependence-supportive behavior, dependent behavior followed by independence-supportive behavior, independent behavior followed by independence-supportive behavior, and independent behavior followed by dependence-supportive behav-

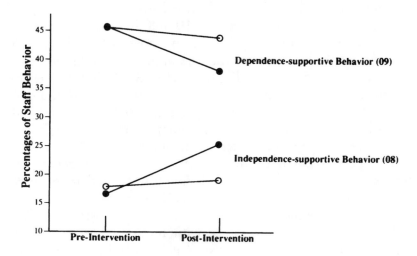

**Behavioral Change from Pre- to Post-Intervention
in the Experimental (●) and Control Group (O)**

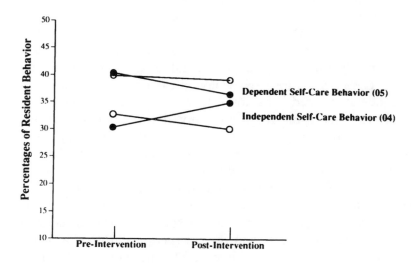

**Behavioral Change from Pre- to Post-Intervention
in Residents Interacting with the Experimental (●)
and Control Group (O)**

Figure 25. Behavior changes in staff and residents.

ior. The dependent variables were conditional probabilities converted to z scores, which were computed using the equation[7] from lag analysis sensu Sackett et al. (1979).

The analysis shows, as expected, a significant interaction effect for group by time by interaction category (see Table 16, part III; and Figure 26). Univariate comparisons show that this effect is due primarily to a decrease in dependence-supportive behavior of staff following independent behavior of residents.

Summary. Comparisons of sequential observations before and after intervention demonstrate, on the level of behavior profiles, an increase in independence-supportive behavior and decrease in dependence-supportive behavior of staff in the experimental group. In addition, there was a change in the behavior of the elderly residents from pre- to postobservation in that they exhibited more independent behavior when interacting with staff from the experimental group.

On the level of interaction patterns, the change from pre- to postintervention was mainly due to a decrease in one interaction pattern in the experimental group, namely independent behavior followed by dependence-supportive behavior. The respective changes in the dependency–support script and independence–support script are in the right direction but not statistically significant.

We can conclude that the training program aimed at changing the behavior of staff in order to produce a change in the dominant interaction pattern, the dependency–support script, in long-term care institutions can be considered successful.

There are several implications of these findings. First, and very important, we now have proof (see page 110) that the temporal behavior patterns suggest a functional relationship between antecedent and consequent behaviors.

Second, the results confirm the malleability of social environmental conditions responsible for dependency in the elderly. Specifically, even long-standing staff behavior can be changed to optimize conditions supporting autonomy of the elderly. Staff, when given the required skills (e.g., insight into aging conditions and helpful behavior strategies), are able and willing to pay attention to and reinforce the strengths and competencies of the

Table 16. *Results of Statistical Analysis: Significant Results from Three Separate MANOVAs with Repeated Measures for Staff Behavior, Resident Behavior, and Interaction Pattern (N = 27)*

Source of Variation	F	df	Effect Size
Staff Behavior, Part I			
Behavior category	149.97**	1, 21	.88
Behavior category × Time	37.25**	1, 21	.64
Behavior category × Time × Group	20.50**	1, 21	.49
Behavior category × Time × Institution	8.62**	2, 21	.49
Behavior category × Group × Institution	8.51**	2, 21	.45
Behavior category × Time × Institution × Group	4.50*	2, 21	.29
Univariate Comparisons			
Independence-supportive behavior	14.3**	1, 21	
Dependence-supportive behavior	10.8**	1, 21	
Resident behavior, Part II			
Behavior category	13.76	1, 21	.39
Behavior category × Time	5.15*	1, 21	.19
Behavior category × Time × Group	7.27**	1, 21	.26
Behavior category × Time × Group × Institution	2.25	2, 21	.17
Univariate Comparisons:			
Independent behavior	9.90**	1, 21	
Interaction Pattern, Part III			
Interaction category	52.86**	3, 19	.89
Institution	10.78**	2, 21	.50
Interaction category × Time	8.45**	3, 19	.57
Interaction category × Institution	3.60*	6, 38	.36
Interaction category × Time × Group	4.67**	3, 19	.42
Interaction category × Time × Group × Institution	2.74*	6, 38	.30
Univariate Comparisons:			
Independent Behavior followed by Dependence-Supportive Behavior	10.0**	1, 21	

Note: MANOVA = multivariate analysis of variance.
*$p < .05$
**$p < .01$

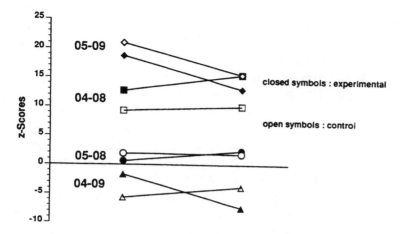

Figure 26. Behavior changes in interaction patterns.

elderly. This autonomy-enhancing perspective is readily adopted and in line with a helping role when helping is understood as "help toward self-help."

It should be noted here that our findings would be stronger if only the state-run nursing home and the geriatric hospital ward had been considered. The religiously affiliated nursing home did not show much change from pre- to postintervention. This is not due to a ceiling effect, that is, staff in this home did behave in a more optimal way to begin with; no, they simply did not profit from training. On neither the behavioral nor the cognitive attitudinal level did this group show much learning.

Although our questionnaire data are difficult to compare – since there were a number of missings in the control group – it can be inferred that cognitive restructuring, emphasizing potential competencies of the elderly, can help staff members to acquire an appropriate care-giving style. When combined with the required skills in communication and behavior management, the independence-supportive interaction pattern can be realized with great effectiveness. We have to acknowledge here that it is not possible to say which component of training was more responsible for the training effects, although the behavioral management component took the largest time and was considered by staff to be the most beneficial segment.

Finally, findings suggest that institutions can provide environments that are both stimulating and protective at the same time (Parmelee & Lawton, 1990). If staff behavior is tailored to the individual competence level of elderly residents – that is, providing security and support only when and where truly needed and otherwise supporting autonomy and stimulation – the elderly resident can compensate for deficits with the help of staff but maintain and even optimize remaining competencies. In this sense, institutions may lose their negative image as "total institutions" (Goffman 1961) and even serve as age-friendly environments allowing for positive aging (Baltes, Wahl, & Reichert, 1991). There is, however, a remaining question as to who decides when and under what circumstances there is to be support for dependency and when there should be demand for or stimulation of independence.

8

Behavioral Dependency and Successful Aging

Dependency: Selective Optimization with Compensation (the Case of Sue)

The last observations point to a larger behavioral system of adaptation within which dependency in old age is located. I have recently made the argument for a third paradigm of behavioral dependency, namely self-regulated dependency. This third paradigm is closely tied to the model of selective optimization with compensation (P. B. Baltes & M. M. Baltes, 1990; Baltes & Carstensen, in press), in which dependency or other forms of performance reduction can have positive adaptive value. The basic assumption of the model is that due to increasing losses in reserves and strengths, the elderly person is faced with the possibility of (a) giving up the activity or domain hampered by loss or weaknesses, (b) compensating for the weaknesses, or (c) becoming increasingly dependent in those weakened or threatened domains so as to free energy for the pursuit of other domains and activities that have higher priority to the elderly person. With this latter strategy, she or he acknowledges losses and makes adjustments accordingly. Which activities to give up, which to maintain, which to become dependent in will vary greatly from person to person, reflecting interindividual differences in preferences, motivations, skills, and so on. Thus, what kind of dependent behaviors an individual would exhibit, to what degree, and in what situations, are subject largely to his or her own life history and experiences, current physical and psychological status, and current environmental conditions.

In the model of selective optimization with compensation, the positive adaptive potential of lowered performance, such as dependency, is highlighted. We argue that effective coordination of three processes, selection, compensation, and optimization, ensures successful aging despite many losses and the diminution in reserve capacities.

Selection is based on the argument that (a) new developmental tasks in old age (elective selection) and (b) a reduced capacity and age-associated losses (loss-based selection) mandate reduction of both activities and domains. Selection, thus, refers to an increasing restriction on domains of functioning as a consequence or in anticipation of losses in personal and environmental resources. Selection may mean avoidance of one domain altogether, or it can mean a restriction of tasks or goals within one domain or a number of domains. Thus, an elderly person experiencing the terminal illness of a spouse might give up sexual activities altogether, might restrict some goals and involvements in the social network at large, but might make no changes in the domains of leisure activities and family. It is the adaptive task of the person to concentrate on and select those domains, tasks, goals, and expectations that are of high priority and involve a convergence of environmental demands, individual motivations, skills, and biological capacity.

Although selection connotes a reduction in the number of high-efficacy domains, tasks, goals, and so on, it can also involve the adoption of new or transformed domains and goals of life. Thus, the person who loses a spouse might deal with the loss by taking over and carrying on his or her political activities and maintaining his or her legacy.

Selection implies that an individual's expectations are readjusted and reassessed. Selection can be proactive or reactive. Selection encompasses both environmental changes (e.g., relocation), active behavior changes (reducing the number of commitments), or passive adjustment (avoiding climbing stairs or allowing somebody to take responsibility). People can proactively monitor their functioning, predict future changes and losses (e.g., death of the spouse) and make efforts to search for tasks and domains that will remain intact after losses. Selection is reactive when unpredicted or sudden changes force the person to make a selection. If a stroke suddenly severely impairs a person, a decision to remain at home might not be viable, but the person can engage in selection processes about which institution is best, how much and what kind of self-care is needed, what type of rehabilitation and what activities to engage in, what television program to watch, when to write a letter, make a telephone call, and so forth.

The adaptive task for the aging individual is to select and concentrate on those domains that are of high priority and that involve a convergence of environmental demands, individual preferences, and biological capacity. Dependent behavior, therefore, could present self-selected adaptive measures by which the elderly uses his or her environment as a way to bolster other still remaining competencies. B. F. Skinner (1983) described an array of environmental aids that he used to maintain and enhance his intellectual performance in old age. Concurrently, however, other domains have to be neglected, resulting possibly in dependent behaviors in those domains. The case of Sue is an example. She has chosen golf and reading and has given up gardening and housework.

The second component, compensation, becomes operative when specific behavioral capacities or skills are lost or reduced below the level required for adequate functioning. The question here is whether the person has other means to reach the same goal or accomplish the same outcome in a specific domain. Losses in specific behavioral capacities loom particularly large when situations and goals require a wide range of activity and a high level of performance (e.g., competitive sports, rush hour traffic, accumulation of daily hassles, and situations that require quick thinking and memorization).

Compensatory efforts can be automatic or planned. If a goal, a domain defined by a large number of activities and means, is well elaborated, the person will not experience much trouble to counterbalance or compensate for a specific behavioral deficiency. If the deficiency is large in scope or if the domains and goals are defined by one or very few activities, compensatory efforts will be more difficult. The real life story about the window box of Brim's father (Brim, 1988) is a concrete illustration of compensation. In order to maintain and optimize his life goal (i.e., to be a farmer), Brim's father compensated for increasing physical impairments by relegating the plowing of the hills to others and concentrating on working his garden; in the end, he tended only his window box and left the hills and the garden in the care of others.

Compensation is not necessarily dependent on already existing behaviors or means. Compensation might sometimes require the acquisition of new skills, of new means not yet in the repertoire. An avid reader of literature who becomes blind might learn braille in order to keep on reading literature or might resort to listening to "books on tape." The element of compensation involves aspects of both the mind and technology. Psychological compensatory efforts include, for example, the use of new mnemonic strategies (including external memory aids) when internal memory mechanics or strategies prove insufficient. The use of a hearing aid is an example of compensation by means of technology. The world of the handicapped is full of technical means that compensate for impairments and make a relatively independent and successful life possible. But human means as well are often needed to compensate. In this sense, the assistance of a hand or arm when walking, the maid who does the cooking, or the companion who does the writing may be compensatory means that enable the elderly to pursue their lives as fully as possible.

To delegate control to others and thereby become perhaps dependent can be a very powerful mechanism to maintain and optimize domains in danger of decline. This mechanism has been labeled by Bandura (1982) as *proxy control.*

An anecdote from a nursing home setting serves as another example. Someone we will call Mr. Jacobs has been living in a nursing home for a short while and has started to avoid carrying out the necessary activities involved in his morning self-care. Instead, a nurse has taken over those tasks and assists him in every step along the way. When the morning self-care tasks are completed, Mr. Jacobs takes his cane, walks to the elevator, rides it down to the lounge area, gets a cigarette and sits down to enjoy watching the busy life in the entrance hall. Asked why he allowed himself to be washed, dressed, and so on, although it was plainly clear that he could do those tasks by himself, he wondered why we did not understand. He told us that if he is completely responsible for his own morning self-care he will not have the time and energy to enjoy what is very important to him: the social world in the entrance hall.

Selection and compensation thus guarantee, foremost, maintenance of functioning. They also help, however, in optimizing functioning. Optimization, the third component factor, reflects the view that old people, too, can grow, can engage in behaviors to enrich and augment reserves or resources, and thus can maximize their chosen life courses with regard to both quantity and quality. Optimization and growth may relate to the further development of already existing goals and expectations (i.e., in the domain of generativity), but may also reflect new goals and expectations in line with developmental tasks of the third phase of life (such as acceptance of one's own mortality).

There seems no doubt that the process of optimization will be contingent to a large extent on stimulating and enhancing environmental conditions. Here society is responsible for such environments. There is little doubt that many elderly, in principle, have the necessary resources and reserves.

Intervention studies on plasticity in the area of cognition, such as memory performance (for review see P. B. Baltes & Lindenberger, 1988), and social behavior, such as dependency, and so on (for reviews see Baltes, 1988, 1995; Mosher-Ashley, 1986–1987) have demonstrated that old people are able to implement optimizing processes. The success of intervention studies, at the same time, illuminates the fact that the elderly often live in a world of deprivation, of "underdemand" rather than "overdemand." In order for optimization to occur, the elderly must have access to an "enriched," perhaps slightly overdemanding environment. Not everybody is ready to forge new terrain and frontiers (Rosenmayr, 1983a,b).

An increase in independence was the goal of the intervention study by Baltes et al. (1994). As was represented in Chapter 7, the aim of the intervention was to change the institutional context from focusing on the dependency–support script to embrace an independence–support script. To activate such a script we designed a training program for caregivers directed at creating greater sensitivity concerning the importance of a balance between dependency and autonomy for the elderly (Parmelee & Lawton, 1990). Results confirm the malleability of social environmental conditions (caregiver behavior) responsible for the dependency in the elderly. Staff, when taught the required skills (e.g., insight into aging conditions and behavior management strategies), are able and willing to pay attention to and reinforce the strengths and competencies of the elderly rather than their weaknesses. The autonomy-enhancing perspective is readily adopted and in line with the helping role when helping is understood as *help toward self-help*.

It is important, however, to realize that optimization in old age is often actualized in a situation of increasing functional losses, and thus what is "optimal" will always be constrained by what is possible. There is not one ideal or standard for what is optimal; it will always be gauged along the possibilities of a person with certain personal and environmental resources and reserves. We contend, thus, that selection and compensation, separately or combined, will have to be enlisted at one point or another during aging to maintain and optimize functioning. B. F. Skinner (1983), for example, in an account of his own aging, gave eloquent advice on intellectual management to preserve and continue high productivity in light of failing reserves.

Although empirical data are not in yet, consideration of this model of successful aging, with its explicit concern for increased selection and compensation, elucidates from yet another perspective *why* dependent behaviors in the elderly should not be seen only as signs of helplessness, lack of control, and dysfunctionality. Dependent behaviors can be functional, and in many instances can provide the elderly with control, access to social partners, and important opportunities to select and compensate.

9

Conclusions and Implications

Behavioral dependency in late life has at least three etiologies: learned helplessness, learned dependency, and selective optimization with compensation. In the first two paradigms, behavioral dependency is socially induced. The environment either expects incompetence and provides help even if it is not needed or wanted, or it is unresponsive and neglectful. This latter environment has been characterized by Seligman as a noncontingent environment that leads to helplessness and ensuing dependency.

In contrast, the low-demanding environment demonstrated in my own research is a contingent environment that is characterized by overcare and results in behavioral dependency. Institutional and community environments do not seem to be characterized only by noncontingency, but are worlds in which the elderly very quickly discriminate between differential consequences for dependent and independent behaviors. It is the dependent, not the independent, behaviors that are instrumental in securing social consequences, attention, and contact. Dependent behaviors are instrumental in exerting control over the social world. Although passive, this control seems to fulfill a very important compensatory function in gaining and securing social contact. In this sense, dependent behaviors are highly functional and adaptive.

In the third paradigm proposed here, behavioral dependency is the outcome of selection by the elderly and is thus self-induced. Due to diverse losses, the elderly are making decisions concerning priority and energy investment. For intervention purposes it seems rather important to find out what kind of dependency is present (see page 28).

There are three aspects in the research on dependency, particularly behavioral dependency, that need highlighting: first, the environmental impact on behavior of the elderly; second, the dialectic between dependency and autonomy; and third, the person–environment fit perspective.

Environmental Impact on Behavior of the Elderly

The presented research has employed convergent operations (experimental, observational, intervention, and interview strategies) to gain a more comprehensive understanding of behavioral dependency in the elderly. Our work has shown that behavioral dependency is not a necessary concomitant of old age. Rather, the environment plays a dominant role in the development and maintenance of dependency in the elderly. We have demonstrated that the dependency–support script and independence–ignore script are basic characteristics of the social world of the elderly.

There is no doubt that the elderly, due to decreasing reserves, are more vulnerable and affected by environmental conditions. The environment will have hindering as well as enhancing effects. But, instead of cultivating the remaining strengths and emphasizing the activation of latent reserves (see experimental findings in Chapters 4 and 7, and Research Question 3), the environment exaggerates the weaknesses by expecting incompetence or incompetence-proneness in the elderly (see observational findings and Research Question 4 in Chapter 7).

Behavioral dependency as a function of differential environmental contingencies has two implications. Since it is the outcome of overcare, there are both a dysfunctional and a functional consequence. It is dysfunctional in that they might accelerate aging decline due to nonuse of still existing skills. Dependent behaviors are functional in serving as an instrument to secure control within the social domain, especially with regard to social contact, a rare commodity particularly in institutions. We have argued previously (Baltes & Reisenzein, 1986) that this congruent contingency between dependent behaviors and environmental consequences challenges the view that dependent behavior in the elderly is predominantly a result of lack of control or self-efficacy, as propagated by a learned helplessness perspective. Instead, dependent behaviors are often an instrument to control specific events, namely social and physical contact and supportive attention. Thus, while the dependency–support script can be interpreted as being a costly reinforcement schedule for "becoming" more and more dependent, it also contains possible gains affiliated with achieving a predictable social world and associated "secondary" benefits.

To prevent a possible misunderstanding of these interpretations, three observations should be mentioned. First, whereas in the present research it has been shown that dependent behavior in the elderly is associated with positive consequences (such as predictable control and social contact), this does not imply that dependent behavior as a whole is desirable. The consequences of dependent behavior also include potential negative consequences, such as a trajectory toward less competence and less autonomy. Second, it is occasionally argued that the instrumental control of dependent self-care shown in the present data implies a "manipulative" and, therefore, undesirable strategy on the part of the elderly. On the one hand, we do not have the data (such as indicators of cognitive measures) to support this conclusion of conscious and instrumental goal-orientation on the part of the elderly. On the other hand, we need to acknowledge that attributing a negative evaluation to the instrumental control characteristic of dependent behavior is somewhat cynical. Any sense of psychological control dealing with the social environment in whatever age group involves a predictable impact of one's behavior on the social partner. Third, it is also suggested that resorting to dependent behavior as the focus of social control is undesirable, that it would be more appropriate to connect social control with independent, autonomous behavior. This seems meaningful in principle. However, because of the factual existence of failing resources in the elderly, this expectation is idealistic. What appears more beneficial is to offer the elderly a sense of control in both realms: dependency and independence. Achieving a good balance between social control in situations of dependence as well as independence is the challenge of the future. Until such a balance is achieved, the fact that the elderly feel a sense of social control following their dependent behavior must be considered a desirable though incomplete characteristic of their social world.

Nevertheless, the experience of control in the context of dependency has two caveats. First, dependent behaviors provide the experience of passive control that, in the long run, might prove as detrimental as the experience of no control. Second, the establishment or arrangement of the behavior–consequence contingencies is dictated by the environment, not chosen by the elderly. In this sense we can speak of dependent behaviors as being adaptive to the environmental constraints or rules. In selecting or preferring one interaction pattern over others and thereby creating a social script, the social environment accepts dependent behavior as appropriate and in line with normative expectations. This suggests a perception of the elderly by their partners as incompetent or, at least, as dependence-prone (Baltes, Wahl, & Reichert, 1991).

When considering the comparative observational data from children and from elderly at home as well as the operant-experimental data from the institutionalized elderly, it seems that it is a systemic assumption of incompetence rather than real incompetence that nourishes the typical interaction patterns in long-term care institutions. Whereas the social partners of children – particularly mothers – tailor their own behavior (dependence- or independence-supportive behavior) to match the child's developmental stage (i.e., the child's competence level), social partners of the elderly are most likely to expect incompetence.

Reichert (1993) has confirmed this suggestion when comparing nurses and educators interacting with elderly people in problem-solving situations. The interactions between nurses and elderly persons are significantly different from those between educators and elderly and characterized by direct and immediate helping behaviors. Karuza et al. (1986) describe such behavior as the result of the medical helping model in which responsibilities are taken over by the environment – that is, by caregivers. The dependency–support script thus describes an overresponsive environment that fosters dependent behaviors at the cost of independent behaviors and is insensitive to a person's remaining strengths.

This view is confirmed further by the attributional style held by the elderly and their social partners with regard to dependent and independent behaviors. When confronting elderly persons and their partners with their respective observed behaviors, Wahl

(1991) found that social partners ascribe responsibility for dependent behaviors to the elderly but attribute independent behavior of the elderly to their own (the social partner's) doing. In contrast, the elderly ascribe independent behavior to themselves but dependent behavior either to illness or to their environment – that is, the behavior of social partners.

Consequently, in both instances of behavioral dependency – as the product of noncontingencies (learned helplessness) or as the result of existing contingencies (learned dependency) – the person is often competent. This has been documented in the case of the elderly by many experimental operant studies (see pages 36–40; for review see Mosher-Ashley, 1986–1987) as well as our ecological intervention data (see pages 131–144) demonstrating modifiability of dependent behaviors. In both cases of behavioral dependency, the environment is the culprit either by being unresponsive or by providing more security and protection than needed. As such, it seems logical to ask for a change in the environment, in order to encourage competencies and independence instead of discouraging them and fostering dependency.

We have demonstrated that such a change can be implemented and evaluated using the third methodological strategy, namely the ecological intervention strategy (Baltes et al., 1994). Using a training program to change the behavior of social partners by teaching them to increase independence-related interaction patterns, we could show that institutional environments can be designed to be stimulating and more demanding, thereby fostering skills and competencies of the elderly. The autonomy-enhancing perspective is readily adopted by staff and in line with their helping role when helping is understood as "help toward self-help." At the same time, however, social partners need to avoid setting up a situation of overdemand. The borders between dependency and independence are not fixed but highly flexible.

Dialectic between Dependency and Independence

Parmelee and Lawton (1990) base the dialectic between dependency and independence on two basic human needs: security and autonomy. The environment is seen to be responsible for providing protection and stimulation. Protection is entailed in the dependency–support script, whereas stimulation requires an independence–support script. We have seen that the dependency–support script is the dominant feature in the world of the elderly, accepted both by social partners and by the elderly themselves. Thus, protection prevails as the overriding concern, and the need of the elderly for security should be more than met.

What about stimulation? We have seen that, in principle, the elderly have reserves that could be stimulated, which would lead to an increase in independence and autonomy. The data show that there are differences in the social worlds, for instance, between institutional and community settings. We have seen that social partners in the community settings do respond to independent behaviors significantly more frequently than do social partners in institutions. The responses are ambivalent, however. In fact, there are more incongruent (dependence-supportive) than congruent (independence-supportive) behaviors following independent behaviors of the elderly in the community.

Why do social partners in the community setting behave in such an ambivalent fashion? It seems to point to a confusion or conflict about how to treat the elderly. Two possible interpretations stand out. On the one hand, there is a disposition toward dependency–support based on a negative aging stereotype. On the other hand, caregivers in the community setting might feel the pressure of social policies (Guillemard, 1992). In Germany, as in the United States, home-based care is associated with social expectations of maintaining independence and preventing institutionalization as long as possible. Thus, caregivers seem to react to two social pressures or systems of expectations: a negative aging stereotype involving expectations of loss of independence in old age, and the present philosophy in social policy associated with home-based care that aims to protect the remaining independence. Whether such an interpretation is valid, however, requires further investigation aimed at uncovering the beliefs of the social partners as they engage in the social transactions surrounding self-care. We have only started in this endeavor (see pages 128–129).

It is important to note that caregiving does not consist of one (independence–support) script or the other (dependency–support) script. Rather, caregiving needs to encompass both in order to allow the elderly to adapt (compensate) and to grow (optimize). In this sense caregiving for the elderly is no different from caregiving for children (Bradley & Caldwell, 1995).

Person–Environment Fit Perspective

The importance of the environment in determining autonomy or security evokes the concept of person–environment fit (Lawton & Nahemow, 1973), or in Kahana's (1982) terms, the congruence–incongruence between the residents' characteristics and those of the environment. Person–environment fit entails reciprocal concurrent influences between the context and the individual over time, with individuals searching for and designing their environment and the environment shaping the individual. The model of Lawton and colleagues (i.e., Lawton & Nahemow, 1973; Lawton, 1987) represents the fit as a linear increase in the relationship between competence and environmental demands; both a low-competent person in a low-demanding environment as well as a highly competent person in a high-demanding environment are likely to experience a high level of well-being and satisfaction. Deviations from the fit lead to negative outcomes, such as boredom in the case of high competence and low demands, and stress in the case of low competence and high demands. Parmelee and Lawton (1990), speaking about a dialectic between the two basic human needs of security and autonomy, argue, therefore, for an environment that is fitted to both strengths and weaknesses of the elderly, one that keeps security (dependence–support) and stimulation (independence–support) in equal focus.

The goal cannot be to design and create *the* optimal environment for all, but rather to design and create tailor-made environments that balance efforts at selection, compensation, and optimization. Because of increasing losses with age, there is often little doubt that support (compensation) is needed in specific areas (selection) in order to maintain or even optimize other areas. A thorough assessment of the competence level of the elderly seems to be the linchpin between security or autonomy. Often no objective assessment of the elderly's competence is made and regularly reassessed after they enter institutions. On the contrary, research in nursing homes suggests that individual assessment of strengths and weaknesses under diverse environmental conditions is often replaced by conventional negative stereotyping and generalized expectations of extant and growing incompetence (Baltes et al., 1991). As long as this is the case, caregivers run the risk of offering excessive care and thus harming rather than helping the elderly.

Environments – the institution, the family, the caregivers, and so on – as well as the elderly themselves would profit from a better fit between competence of the elderly and the helping response from the environment. For the social partners, it seems particularly important to scrutinize their compensatory efforts in their care of the elderly for risks of overcompensation and overprotection with the associated lack of opportunity for maintenance and optimization of effective functioning.

The elderly person, too, has a specifically difficult task: At a time of increasing biological vulnerability demands due to developmental tasks of old age – e.g., adjustment to retirement and other social losses, to increasing health impairments, and to one's mortality – require strengths and adaptation. Moreover, the occurrence of most of these events is not under human control, and thus, although normative they are often not predictable nor controllable. On the one hand, autonomy and agency are asked for to deal with these tasks. On the other hand, given the increasing vulnerability, the elderly person must be able to transform agency, when and where needed, into behavioral dependency, delegating control in order to adapt successfully. For the elderly person staying in control and mastering aging is like walking a tightrope.

10

Outlook

After summarizing my empirical inquiry into the study of the social and social-interactive conditions surrounding the origins, maintenance, and transformation of autonomy and dependency in old age, I feel a sense of ambivalence, a sense of relief mixed with emptiness. Summarizing a career-long research program feels like separating from, even losing, a child that one has nourished, fostered, and loved and cannot replace. Presenting the intricacies and many interdependencies of this research program, not least because of the intertwining of several methodologies, was no easy task. Therefore, I would not be surprised if the reader developed some irritation about my decision to go into such detail, particularly regarding the format of observational methodology and its statistical analysis.

In this brief outlook, therefore, I will attempt to distance myself somewhat from the specifics of the empirical inquiries and guide my thoughts to the larger intellectual and social policy agenda within which the present program of research on the many faces of dependency in old age can be placed. In particular, I offer some concluding observations on two topics: (1) research and policy on human aging and (2) implications for psychological and sociological research on the nature of social interdependence.

Implications for the Nature of Human Aging and Intervention

Recent decades have witnessed the rapid expansion of gerontology as an interdiscipline as well as a collection of disciplinary specializations. Among the central issues were questions about the plasticity of the aging process and the search for interconnections between levels of analysis, for instance, among descriptive, explanatory, and interventive attempts. In fact, for a number of gerontologists, the creation of this intersect of description, explanation, and intervention has become a hallmark of their commitment to the field. In general, it was not sufficient to try to understand the sources and mechanisms of aging. The intellectual motivation to move beyond the purely scientific task and use the acquired knowledge to optimize the aging process often seemed so strong that one was willing to argue for particular interventions even before the answers to "basic knowledge" questions were available.

In the two decades of the life of the present research program I felt this tension between knowledge generation and knowledge application very intensely. Often, I refused to propagate particular intervention efforts against the personal advice of others whom I much admire. It took a long time until I was sufficiently satisfied to open the window toward application.

Now, I do believe that the wait and the search for the interconnections among description, explanation, and intervention have been worthwhile. And the long wait has also altered my view not only about what is possible and not possible, but also about the varying ramifications of dependent behavior. Yes, the data do support the view that a sizeable portion of dependency in old age is conditioned by social factors. Aging stereotypes and the behavior of social partners of elderly persons do set constraints and define interpersonal scripts that move older persons to more dependency than is biologically and psychologically necessary.

However, the data also support the view that not everything in aging stereotypes and social control directed at dependency is bad and dysfunctional. On the contrary, an equally important part of the story is that social support of and stimulation toward dependency is functional and in the interest of the older person. Let me repeat two of these reasons. First, by receiving help older persons free up resources for those domains of functioning that give them opportunities for personal satisfaction and even growth. Second, many of the positive social contacts that older persons receive are intimately tied to dependency. Without the dependency–support script, older persons would have less control over their social environment. Any view focusing on only one face of dependency falls short and misleads the effort at intervention. An interesting aside is that this multifaceted picture of dependency turns out to be the major message of the psychodynamic and trait psychology approach toward dependency as well (Bornstein, 1993).

These are new insights into the social nature of human aging that harbor specific suggestions for designing a better future of old age. In designing a better culture of old age, we cannot proceed only on the assumption that older individuals have the plasticity to remain autonomous and independent. In order for the available individual potential (plasticity) to be used effectively for the benefit of older persons and their struggle for meaning of life, this remaining plasticity needs to be invested into those sectors of life and domains of functioning that make their living worthwhile. And because of large individual and cultural differences, it is necessary to generate contexts of living and social support that recognize losses in capacity but at the same time permit individuation and selective optimization.

In this sense, the present research program has at least two messages that transcend its substantive territory, that is, the study of dependency in old age. The first message is to conduct research on aging which integrates descriptive, explanatory, and intervention efforts. The second is to be reflective about intervention efforts based solely on optimism and the latent potential of older persons. Intervention efforts need to recognize at least two aspects. Older individuals exhibit dramatic individual differences and, therefore, treating the older person as a member of a single category is highly inappropriate. What is necessary is to keep in the foreground the person- and context-specific conditions of aging individuals.

Furthermore, before moving to intervention – such as pushing an older person to raise the level of functioning in a given domain because it is possible in principle – careful research needs to be conducted into the question whether losses in functioning have positive consequences for the conduct and management of life in old age. There are widespread and robust aging-associated losses in biological and psychological potential which cannot be easily modified. Because of multifunctionality, these seemingly dysfunctional states actually may be the key ingredients for maintaining a purpose in life and creating new forms of social embeddedness. As there are many faces to dependency, and some features of dependency are behavior-enhancing, I suggest that there are many faces to other, so-called gerontological declines and interventions therein as well. Pushing older individuals in every level and domain to high performances is likely to be counterproductive by ignoring the behavior-enhancing effect of reduced efficacy and output.

Implications for the Study of Social Embeddedness and Social Dynamics

What about implications for other fields of social inquiry? Thus far in the book I have only fleetingly attempted to elucidate the implications of this program of research for the study of social dynamics and social embeddedness in general. Therefore, as a conclusion to this book I will at least mention a few of the possibilities.

The many faces of dependency are not only an issue in old age. On the contrary, I argue that similar issues apply to all phases of life. Being dependent, withdrawing temporarily or long-term from autonomy and independence, arranging for the proper balance between dependency and autonomy, is likely a topic in earlier age phases as well (Baltes & Silverberg, 1992). And from a methodological point of view, I argue that multifunctionality of interpersonal relations is understudied, especially due to a lack of "convergent operations" (Baer, 1973) in this strand of work. I suggest, therefore, that research in infancy, childhood, adolescence, adulthood, or work on marriage and interpersonal relations, equally attempts to employ the kind of methodological paradigms used in the present work. We know too little about the multifunctionality and complementarity of dependent behaviors, and their systemic combination with independence and autonomy. Here lies a field which is largely underexplored, perhaps in part because the triangulation of descriptive, explanatory, and interventive research is time- and energy-consuming and easily overtaxes our motivational and economic resources.

Another topic of much interest is the question about the interconnection between behavioral and cognitive approaches, to the study of the many faces of social dynamics and social embeddedness. Much of what we know about the social fabric of human behavior is based on cognitive approaches including such theoretical frameworks as social cognition and symbolic interactionism. What I was able to demonstrate in the present program of research is that our personal, intuitive, and cognitive insights into the nature of social transactions do not necessarily reflect their objective nature in reality. A case in point is the research on control. So far, much of our knowledge about primary and secondary control in humans relies on cognitive research programs. I argue that to obtain a full picture, we need to be guided not only by what people think but also what they do without knowing (awareness) – why they behave the way they do. There are limitations to our cognitive access to principles of multicausality and multifunctionality.

Take the role of the dependency–support script for the control and initiation of social interactions on the part of older persons as an example. My colleagues and I were able to show that being dependent is a major condition for generating social transactions that extend beyond the sheer topic of dependency-related care. It is in this context that older persons generate and experience contingencies that increase their level of social influence. In this context, multicausality and multifunctionality reigned supreme. Such information is difficult to obtain from cognitively motivated programs of research. This insight was possible only because of the use of multiple behavioral observations and time-lagged conditional probabilites of actual behavioral events. By plotting multiple behaviors of the interacting partners over time, it was possible to detect new forms of contingencies which, if interpreted in the framework of social learning theory, resulted in a new window on the nature of the social transactions between older persons and their caregiving partners.

The present work, then, carries implications that transcend the specific scope of this book; implications for the study of human aging in general, as well as for the psychological study of social structure and function. It is in this spirit that I hope for a readership which includes fellow gerontologists but also scholars who view the study of dependency in old age as a sample case for more general issues of developmental, social, and clinical psychology.

Notes

CHAPTER 5

1. The results show a main effect for behavior category (F (4, 124) = 79.34, p < .001; w^2 = .64), no main effect for length of institutionalization (F (3, 31) = 1.21, p = .324), and no interaction effect (F (12, 124) = .64, p = .802).

   The results for staff show a significant main effect for behavior category (F (4, 124) = 27.62; p = .001; w^2 = .37), no main effect for length of institutionalization (F (3, 31) = 1.96, p = .141), and no interaction effect (F (12, 124) = 1.12, p = .350).

2. After missing data had been estimated by means of multiple regression, homogeneity of variances was tested via a conservative F-test. The results show a main effect for behavior category (F (1, 36) = 175.8; p < .001; w^2 = 0.73). In addition, there was a significant interaction effect between behavior category and length of institutionalization (F (1, 36) = 4.35; p < .01; w^2 = .006). Since this latter effect accounted for only 0.6% of the variance it will not be discussed any further. No other main or interaction effects were obtained.

3. Applying a multivariate procedure with repeated measurements on the last two factors, the results show main effects for type of behavior (F (10, 67) = 11,850.18, p < .001) and for form of behavior (F (5, 72) = 64,707.23, p < .001). All interaction effects are significant: Type × Home (F (10, 67) = 4.89; p < .001); Form × Home (F (5, 72) = 9.03; p < .001); Type × Form (F (46, 31) = 15,462.76; p < .001); and Type × Form × Home (F (46, 31) = 3.49; p < .001). Planned comparisons were used for significance testing.

CHAPTER 6

4. Chi-square (1, 78) = 13.57, p < .01; chi-square (1, 48) = 3.26, and chi-square (1, 52) = 2.23.

CHAPTER 7

5. This coding of the situation was introduced to find out whether interaction patterns differed between these situations. This was not the case. There was

no difference in the dominance of the dependency–support script between these situations (see Wahl & Baltes, 1992).

6. Observational procedure was largely the same as used in our previous studies. Differences are described here.

7. The general equation and an example for the behavior sequence 04–08 are

$$z = \frac{Po - Pe}{\sqrt{\dfrac{Pe\,(1 - Pe)\,(1 - Pa)}{N_a}}}$$

$$z = \frac{p\,(08/04) - p\,(08)}{\sqrt{\dfrac{p\,(08)\,(1 - p\,(08)\,(1 - p\,(04))}{N\,(04)}}}$$

where
z = z values,
Po = conditional observed probability,
Pe = base probability of consequent behavior,
Pa = probability of antecedent behavior,
N_a = observed frequency of antecedent behavior.

References

Abramson, L. Y., Seligman, M. E. P., & Teasdale, J. Y. (1978). Learned helplessness in humans: Critique and reformulation. *Journal of Abnormal Psychology, 87,* 49–74.

Ainsworth, M. D. S. (1969). Object relations, dependency, and attachment: A theoretical review of the infant–mother relationship. *Child Development, 40,* 969–1025.

(1972). Attachment and dependency: A comparison. In J. L. Gewirtz (Ed.), *Attachment and dependency* (pp. 97–137). New York: Wiley.

Akhtar, A. J., Broe, G. A., Crombie, G. A., McLean, W. M. R., & Andrews, G. W. (1973). Disability and dependence in the elderly at home. *Age and Aging, 2,* 102–111.

Allison, P. A., & Liker, J. K. (1982). Analyzing sequential categorial data on dyadic interaction: A comment on Gottman. *Psychological Bulletin, 91,* 393–403.

Azuma, H. (1984) Secondary control as a heterogeneous category. *American Psychologist, 39,* 970–971.

Baer, D. J. (1973). The control of developmental processes: Why wait? In J. R. Nesselroade & H. W. Reese (Eds.), *Life-span developmental psychology: Methodological issues* (pp. 187–193). New York: Academic Press.

Baltes, M. M. (1979). Comparing interaction patterns for highly independent and highly dependent residents. Unpublished analysis. The Pennsylvania State University.

(1982). Environmental factors in dependency among nursing home residents: A social ecology analysis. In T. A. Wills (Ed.), *Basic processes in helping relationships* (pp. 405–425). New York: Academic Press.

(1987). Erfolgreiches Altern als Ausdruck von Verhaltenskompetenz und Umweltqualität [Successful aging as a product of behavioral competence and environmental quality]. In C. Niemitz (Ed.), *Der Mensch im Zusammenspiel von Anlage und Umwelt [Humans as product of heredity and environment]* (pp. 353–376). Frankfurt: Suhrkamp.

(1988). The etiology and maintenance of dependency in the elderly: Three phases of operant research. *Behavior Therapy, 19,* 301–319.

(1995). Dependencies in old age: Gains and losses. *Current Directions in Psychological Science, 4,* 14–19.

Baltes, M. M., & Barton, E. M. (1977). New approaches toward aging: A case for the operant model. *Educational Gerontology: An International Quarterly, 2,* 383–405.

(1979). Behavioral analysis of aging: A review of the operant model and research. *International Journal of Behavioral Development, 2,* 297–320.

Baltes, M. M., Barton, E. M., Orzech, M. J., & Lago, D. (1983). Die Mikroökologie von Bewohnern und Personal: Eine Behavior-Mapping Studie im Altenheim [The micro-ecology of residents and staff: A behavior mapping study in a nursing home]. *Zeitschrift für Gerontologie, 16,* 18–26.

Baltes, M. M., Burgess, R. L., & Stewart, R. (1980). Independence and dependence in self-care behaviors in nursing home residents: An operant-observational study. *International Journal of Behavioral Development, 3,* 489–500.

Baltes, M. M., & Carstensen, L. A. (in press). The process of successful aging. *Ageing and Society.*

Baltes, M. M., Honn, S., Barton, E. M., Orzech, M. J., & Lago, D. (1983). On the social ecology of dependence and independence in elderly nursing home residents: A replication and extension. *Journal of Gerontology, 38,* 556–564.

Baltes, M. M., Kindermann, T., & Reisenzein, R. (1986). Die Beobachtung von unselbständigem und selbständigem Verhalten in einem Berliner Altenheim: Die soziale Umwelt als Einflussgrösse [Observation of dependent and independent behavior in two Berlin nursing homes: The role of the social environment]. *Zeitschrift für Gerontologie, 19,* 14–24.

Baltes, M. M., Kindermann, T., Reisenzein, R., & Schmid, U. (1987). Further observational data on the behavioral and social world of institutions for the aged. *Psychology and Aging, 2,* 390–403.

Baltes, M. M., & Lascomb, S. L. (1975). Creating a healthy institutional environment: The nurse as a change agent. *International Journal of Nursing Studies, 12,* 5–12.

Baltes, M. M., Mayr, U., Borchelt, M., Maas, J., & Wilms, H.-U. (1993). Everyday competence in old and very old age: An inter-disciplinary perspective. *Ageing and Society, 13,* 657–680.

Baltes, M. M., Neumann, E.-M., & Zank, S. (1994). Maintenance and rehabilitation of independence in old age: An intervention program for staff. *Psychology and Aging, 9,* 179–188.

Baltes, M. M., & Reisenzein, R. (1986). The social world in long-term care institutions: Psychosocial control toward dependency. In

M. M. Baltes & P. B. Baltes (Eds.), *The psychology of control and aging* (pp. 315–343). Hillsdale, N.J.: Erlbaum.

Baltes, M. M., Reisenzein, R., & Kindermann, T. (1985). Dependence in institutionalized children: An age-comparative study. Paper presented at the ISSBD Meeting, July, Tours, France.

Baltes, M. M., & Silverberg, S. B. (1994). The dynamics between dependency and autonomy: Illustrations across the life span. In D. L. Featherman, R. M. Lerner, & M. Perlmutter (Eds.), *Life-span development and behavior,* Vol. 12 (pp. 41–90). Hillsdale, N.J.: Erlbaum.

Baltes, M. M., & Skinner, E. A. (1983). Cognitive performance deficits and hospitalization: Learned helplessness, instrumental passivity, or what? Comment on Raps, Peterson, Jonas, and Seligman. *Journal of Personality and Social Psychology, 45,* 1013–1016.

Baltes, M. M., & Wahl, H.-W. (1992). The dependency-support script in institutions: Generalization to community settings. *Psychology and Aging, 7,* 409–418.

Baltes, M. M., Wahl, H.-W., & Reichert, M. (1991). Institutions and successful aging for the elderly? *Annual Review of Gerontology and Geriatrics, 11,* 311–337.

Baltes, M. M., & Zerbe, M. B. (1976a). Independence training in nursing home residents. *The Gerontologist, 16,* 428–432.

(1976b). Reestablishing self-feeding in a nursing home setting. *Nursing Research, 25,* 24–26.

Baltes, P. B. (1987). Theoretical propositions of life-span developmental psychology: On the dynamics between growth and decline. *Developmental Psychology, 23,* 611–626.

Baltes, P. B., & Baltes, M. M. (1990). Psychological perspectives on successful aging: The model of selective optimization with compensation. In P. B. Baltes & M. M. Baltes (Eds.), *Successful aging: Perspectives from the behavioral sciences* (pp. 1–34). Cambridge: Cambridge University Press.

Baltes, P. B., & Goulet, L. R. (1971). Exploration of developmental variables by manipulation and simulation of age differences in behavior. *Human Development, 14,* 149–170.

Baltes, P. B., & Lindenberger, U. (1988). On the range of cognitive plasticity in old age as a function of experience: 15 years of intervention research. *Behavior Therapy, 19,* 283–300.

Baltes, P. B., Reese, H. W., & Lipsitt, L. P. (1980). Life-span developmental psychology. *Annual Review of Psychology, 31,* 65–110.

Baltes, P. B., Reese, H. W., & Nesselroade, J. R. (1977). *Life-span developmental psychology: Introduction to research methods.* Monterey, Calif.: Brooks/Cole.

Bandura, A. (1977). Self-efficacy: Toward a unifying theory of behavioral change. *Psychological Review, 84,* 191–215.

(1982). Self-efficacy mechanism in human agency. *American Psychologist, 37*, 122–147.

Bandura, A., & Walters, R. H. (1963). *Social learning and personality development.* New York: Holt, Rinehart & Winston.

Barker, R. G. (1968). *Ecological psychology.* Stanford, Calif.: Stanford University Press.

Barton, E. M. (1978). The social ecology of the nursing home: A naturalistic study of staff reinforcement contingencies for resident behavior. *Dissertation Abstracts International, 39,* 950B.

Barton, E. M., Baltes, M. M., & Orzech, M. J. (1980). On the etiology of dependence in nursing home residents during morning care: The role of staff behavior. *Journal of Personality and Social Psychology, 38,* 423–431.

Beller, E. K. (1957). Dependency and autonomous achievement striving related to orality and anality in early childhood. *Child Development, 28,* 287–315.

Bickel, H., & Jaeger, I. (1986). Die Inanspruchnahme von Heimen im Alter [The use of nursing homes in old age]. *Zeitschrift für Gerontologie, 19,* 30–39.

Blenkner, R. (1969). The normal dependencies of aging. In R. A. Kalish (Ed.), *The dependencies of old people* (pp. 27–37). Ann Arbor: Institute of Gerontology, University of Michigan.

Blos, P. (1967). The second individuation process. *Psychoanalytic Study of the Child, 22,* 162–186.

Bornstein, R. F. (1992). The dependent personality: Developmental, social, and clinical perspectives. *Psychological Bulletin, 112,* 3–23.

(1993). *The dependent personality.* New York: Guilford.

Bortz, W. M. (1989). Re-defining human aging. *Journal of the American Geriatric Society, 37,* 1092–1096.

(1993). The physics of frailty. *Journal of the American Geriatric Society, 41,* 1004–1008.

Bowlby, J. (1969). *Attachment and loss,* Vol. 1. New York: Basic Books.

Bradley, R. H., & Caldwell, B. M. (1995). Caregiving and the regulation of child growth and development: Describing proximal aspects of caregiving systems. *Developmental Review, 15,* 38–85.

Brandtstädter, J., & Renner, G. (1990). Tenacious goal pursuit and flexible goal adjustment: Explication and age-related analysis of assimilative and accommodative strategies of coping. *Psychology and Aging, 5,* 58–67.

Brandtstädter, J., Wentura, D., & Greve, W (1993). Adaptive resources of the aging self: Outlines of an emergent perspective. *International Journal of Behavioral Development, 16,* 323–349.

Brim, O. G., Jr. & Ryff, C. D. (1980). On the properties of life events. In P. B. Baltes & O. G. Brim, Jr. (Eds.), *Life-span development and behavior,* Vol. 3 (pp. 368–388). New York: Academic Press.

Brim, O. G., Jr. (1988). Losing and winning: The nature of ambition in everyday life. *Psychology Today, 9,* 48–52.

Brock, D. B., Guralnik, J. M., & Brody, J. A. (1990). Demography and epidemiology of aging in the United States. In E. L. Schneider & J. W. Rowe (Eds.), *Handbook of the biology of aging* (pp. 3–23). San Diego, Calif.: Academic Press.

Cairns, R. B. (1972). Attachment and dependency. A psychological and social learning synthesis. In J. L. Gewirtz (Ed.), *Attachment and dependency* (pp. 29–95). New York: Wiley.

Callahan, C. M. (1992). Psychiatric symptoms in elderly patients due to medications. In J. W. Rowe & J. C. Ahronheim (Eds.), *Annual review of gerontology and geriatrics: Focus on medications and the elderly,* Vol. 12 (pp. 41–75). New York: Springer.

Clark, M. (1969). Cultural values and dependency in later life. In R. A. Kalish (Ed.), *The dependencies of old people* (pp. 59–72). Ann Arbor: Institute of Gerontology, University of Michigan.

Cohen, J. (1960). A coefficient of agreement for nominal scales. *Educational and Psychological Measurement, 20,* 37–46.

Collopy, B. J. (1988). Autonomy in long-term care: Some crucial distinctions. *The Gerontologist, 28,* 10–27.

(1990). Ethical dimensions of autonomy in long-term care. *Generations. Journal of The American Society of Aging, 14* (Supplement), 9–12.

Cooper, B. (1984). Home and away: The disposition of mentally ill old people in an urban population. *Social Psychiatry, 19,* 187–196.

Czaja, S. J., Weber, R. A., & Nair, S. N. (1993) A human factors analysis of ADL activities: A capability-demand approach. *Journal of Gerontology, 48* (Special Issue), 44–48.

Dzaman, B. C. (1983). *Staff interaction with a chronically hospitalized psychiatric population: The creation and maintenance of dependency.* Unpublished doctoral dissertation, University of Maryland, College Park.

Erikson, E. H. (1963). *Childhood and society.* 2nd ed. New York: W. W. Norton.

Exton-Smith, A. N., & Evans, J. G. (Eds.) (1977). *Care of the elderly: Meeting the challenge of dependencies.* New York: Academic Press.

Fisher, J. E., & Carstensen, L. L. (1990). Generalized effects of skills training among older adults. *The Clinical Gerontologist, 9,* 91–107.

Franz, C. E., & White, K. M. (1985). Individuation and attachment in personality development: Extending Erikson's theory. *Journal of Personality, 53,* 224–256.

Freud, A. (1958). Adolescence. *Psychoanalytic Study of the Child, 13,* 255–278.

Gallagher, D., Thompson, L. W., & Levy, S. M. (1980). Clinical psychological assessment of older adults. In L. W. Poon (Ed.), *Aging in the 1980s* (pp. 19–40). New York: American Psychological Association.

Gewirtz, J. L. (Ed.). (1972). *Attachment and dependency.* New York: Wiley.

Gilligan, C. (1982a). Adult development and women's development: Arrangements for a marriage. In T. Z. Giele (Ed.), *Women in the middle years: Current knowledge and directions for future research and policy* (pp. 89–114). New York: Wiley.

(1982b). *In a different voice.* Cambridge, Mass.: Harvard University Press.

Goffman, E. (1960). Characteristics of total institutions. In M. R. Stein, A. J. Violich, & D. M. White (Eds.), *Identity and anxiety: Survival of the person in mass society.* New York: Free Press.

(1961). *Asylums: Essays on the social situation of mental patients and other inmates.* Garden City, N.Y.: Doubleday.

Goldfarb, A. I. (1969). The psychodynamics of dependency and the search for aid. In R. A. Kalish (Ed.), *The dependencies of old people* (pp. 1–15). Ann Arbor: Institute of Gerontology, University of Michigan.

Gottman, J. M. (1979) Time-series analysis of continuous data in dyads. In M. E. Lamb, S. G. Suomi, & G. R. Stephenson (Eds.), *Social interaction analysis: Methodological issues.* Madison: University of Wisconsin Press.

Greenberg, R. P., & Bornstein, R. F. (1988a). The dependent personality: I. Risk for physical disorders. *Journal of Personality Disorders, 2,* 126–135.

(1988b). The dependent personality: II. Risk for physical disorders. *Journal of Personality Disorders, 2,* 136–143.

Guillemard, A.-M. (1992). Europäische Perspektiven der Alternspolitik [European perspectives of politics in aging]. In P. B. Baltes & J. Mittelstrass (Eds.), *Zukunft des Alterns und gesellschaftliche Entwicklung* [Future of aging and societal development] (pp. 614–639). Berlin: De Gruyter.

Guralnik, J. M., & Simonsick, E. M. (1993). Physical disability in older Americans. *Journal of Gerontology, 48* (Special Issue), 3–10.

Hartup, W. W. (1963). Dependency and independence. In H. W. Stevenson (Ed.), *Child psychology: The 62nd yearbook of the National Society for the Study of Education* Part 1 (pp. 333–363). Chicago: University of Chicago Press.

Hauser, P. B. (1976). Aging and world-wide population change. In R. H. Binstock & E. Shanas (Eds.), *Handbook of aging and the social sciences* (pp. 58–86). New York: Van Nostrand Reinhold.

Heathers, G. (1953). Emotional dependence and independence in a physical threat situation. *Child Development, 24,* 169–179.

Heckhausen, J., & Schulz, R. (1993). Optimization by selection and compensation: Balancing primary and secondary control in life span development. *International Journal of Behavioral Development, 16,* 287–303.

Hing, E. (Ed.) (1987) *Vital and health statistics.* (Series 13, No. 51). Washington, D.C.: U.S. Government Printing Office.

Hofland, B. F. (1990). Introduction. Autonomy and long-term care practice. *Generations, 14* (Supplement), 5–8.

Hollenbeck, A. R. (1978). Problems of reliability in observational research. In G. P. Sackett (Ed.), *Observing behavior* (pp. 79–98). Baltimore: University Park Press.

Hoyer, W. J. (1974). Aging as intra-individual change. *Developmental Psychology, 10,* 821–826.

Hull, C. L. (1943). *Principles of behavior.* New York: Appleton-Century-Crofts.

Hunter, S., & Sundel, M. (1989) *Midlife myths.* Newbury Park, Calif.: Sage Publications.

Hussian, R. A. (1981). *Geriatric psychology: A behavioral perspective.* New York: Van Nostrand Reinhold.

Hussian, R. A., & Brown, D. C. (1987). Use of two-dimensional grid patterns to limit hazardous ambulation in demented patients. *Journal of Gerontology, 42, 558–560.*

Ittelson, W. H., Rivlin, L. S., & Proshansky, H. M. (1970). The use of behavioral maps in environmental psychology. In H. M. Proshansky, W. H. Ittelson, & L. S. Rivlin (Eds.), *Environmental psychology: Man and his physical setting* (pp. 658–668). New York: Holt, Rinehart & Winston.

Johnson, P. (1989). The structured dependency of the elderly: A critical note. In M. Jeffers (Ed.), *Growing old in the twentieth century* (pp. 62–72). London: Routledge.

Kagan, J. M. (1971). *Change and continuity in infancy.* New York: Wiley.

Kahana, E. (1982). A congruence model of person–environment interaction. In M. P. Lawton, P. B. Windley, & T. O. Byerts (Eds.), *Aging and the environment* (pp. 97–121). New York: Springer.

Kalish, R. A. (Ed.). (1969). *The dependencies of old people.* Ann Arbor: Institute of Gerontology, University of Michigan.

Karuza, J., Rabinowitz, V. D., & Zevon, M. A. (1986). Implications of control and responsibility on helping the aged. In M. M. Baltes & P. B. Baltes (Eds.), *The psychology of control and aging* (pp. 373–396). Hillsdale, N.J.: Lawrence Erlbaum Associates.

Kastenbaum, R., & Candy, S. E. (1973). The 4% fallacy: A methodological and empirical critique of extended care facility population statistics. *International Journal of Aging and Human Development, 4,* 15–21.

Katz, S., Ford, A. B., Moskowitz, R. W., Jackson, B. A., & Jaffe, M. W. (1963). Studies of illness in the aged. *Journal of the American Medical Association, 185,* 914–919.

Kindermann, T. (1993). Fostering independence in mother–child interaction: Longitudinal changes in contingency patterns as children grow competent in developmental tasks. *International Journal of Behavioral Development, 16,* 513–535.

Kuhl, J. (1981). Motivational and functional helplessness: The moderating effect of state versus action orientation. *Journal of Personality and Social Psychology, 40,* 155–170.

(1986). Aging and models of control: The hidden costs of wisdom. In M. M. Baltes & P. B. Baltes (Eds.), *The psychology of control and aging* (pp. 1–34). Hillsdale, N.J.: Erlbaum.

Kuypers, J. A., & Bengtson, V. L. (1973). Social breakdown and competence: A model of normal aging. *Human Development, 16,* 181–201.

LaForge, R. G., Spector, W. D., & Sternberg, J. (1992). The relationship of vision and hearing impairment to one-year mortality and functional decline. *Journal of Aging and Health, 4,* 126–148.

Lair, T., & Lefkowitz, D. (1990). *Mental health and functional health* (Publication No. PHS 90-3470). National Medical Expenditure Research. Rockville, Md.: Public Health Service.

Langer, E. J. (1979). The illusion of incompetence. In L. C. Perlmuter & R. A. Monty (Eds.), *Choice and perceived control* (pp. 301–313). Hillsdale, N.J.: Erlbaum.

(1983). *The psychology of control.* New York: Sage.

Langer, E. J., & Rodin, J. (1976). The effects of choice and enhanced personal responsibility for the aged: A field experiment in an institutional setting. *Journal of Personality and Social Psychology, 34,* 191–198.

Lawton, M. P. (1987). Environment and the satisfaction of the aging. In L. L. Carstensen & B. A. Edelstein (Eds.), *Handbook of clinical gerontology* (pp. 33–40). New York: Pergamon Press.

Lawton, M. P., & Brody, E. M. (1969). Assessment of older people: Self-maintaining and instrumental activities of daily living. *Gerontologist, 9,* 179–185.

Lawton, M. P., & Nahemow, L. (1973). Ecology and the aging process. In C. Eisdorfer & M. P. Lawton (Eds.), *Psychology of adult development and aging* (pp. 619–674). Washington, DC: American Psychological Association.

Lefcourt, M. M. (1976). *Locus of control: Current trends in theory and research.* Hillsdale, N.J.: Erlbaum.

Lester, P. B., & Baltes, M. M. (1978). Functional interdependence of the social environment and the behavior of the institutionalized aged. *Journal of Gerontological Nursing, 4,* 23–27.

Linden, M., Gilberg, R., Horgas, A., & Steinhagen-Thiessen, E. (in press). Die Inanspruchnahme medizinischer und pflegerischer Hilfe im hohen Alter [The use of medical help and care in old age]. In K.-U. Mayer & P. B. Baltes (Eds.), *Die Berliner Altersstudie* [The Berlin Aging Study]. Berlin: De Gruyter.

Maccoby, E. E. (1980). *Social development.* New York: Harcourt Brace Jovanovich.

Maccoby, E. E., & Masters, J. C. (1970). Attachment and dependency. In P. H. Mussen (Ed.), *Carmichael's manual of child psychology,* 3rd ed. Vol. 2 (pp. 73–157). New York: Wiley.

Maddox, G. L. (1984). Aging people and aging population: A framework for decision making. In H. Thomas & G. L. Maddox (Eds.), *New perspectives on old age: A message to decision-makers* (pp. 19–30). New York: Springer.

Matras, J. (1989). Dependency, obligations and entitlements. In J. Matras (Ed.), *A new sociology of aging, the life course, and the elderly* (pp. 260–295). Englewood Cliffs, N.J.: Prentice-Hall.

McCall, R. B. (1977). Challenges to a science of developmental psychology. *Child Development, 48,* 333–344.

Mikulic, M. A. (1971). Reinforcement of independent and dependent patient behavior by nursing personnel: An exploratory study. *Nursing Research, 20,* 162–165.

Moos, R. (1976). *The human context: Environmental determinants of behavior.* New York: John Wiley.

Moos, R. H., & Lembke, S. (1985). Specialized living environments for older people. In J. E. Birren & K. W. Schaie (Eds.), *Handbook of the psychology of aging,* 2nd ed. (pp. 864–889). New York: Van Nostrand Reinhold.

Mosher-Ashley, P. M. (1986–1987). Procedural and methodological parameters in behavioral-gerontological research: A review. *International Journal of Aging and Human Development, 24,* 189–229.

Munnichs, J. M. A., & van den Heuvel, W. J. A. (Eds.). (1976). *Dependency or interdependency in old age.* The Hague, Netherlands: Martinus Nijhoff.

Murphy, L. B. (1962). *The widening world of childhood.* New York: Basic Books.

Neumann, E.-M., Zank, S., Tzschätzsch, K., & Baltes, M. M. (1994). Selbständigkeit im Alter [Autonomy in old age]. 2 vols. Bern: Huber.

Palmore, E. (1977). Facts on aging: A short quiz. *Gerontologist, 17,* 315–320.

  (1981). The facts on aging quiz: Part two. *Gerontologist, 21,* 431–437.

Parmelee, P. A., & Lawton, M. P. (1990). The design of special environments for the aged. In J. E. Birren & K. W. Schaie (Eds.), *Handbook of the psychology of aging,* 3rd ed. (pp. 464–488). New York: Academic Press.

Parr, J. (1980). The interaction of persons and living environments. In L. W. Poon (Ed.), *Aging in the 1980s* (pp. 393–406). Washington, D.C.: American Psychological Association.

Patterson, G. R. (1982). *Coercive family process*. Eugene, Ore.: Castalia.

Patterson, R. L., & Jackson, G. M. (1980). Behavior modification with the elderly. In M. Hersen, R. M. Eisler, & P. Miller (Eds.), *Progress in behavior modification*, Vol. 9 (pp. 205–239). New York: Academic Press.

   (1981). Behavioral approaches to gerontology. In L. Michelson, M. Hersen, & S. Turner (Eds.), *Future perspectives in behavior therapy* (pp. 293–313). New York: Plenum Press.

Peterson, L. C., & Raps, C. S. (1984). Helplessness and hospitalization: More remarks. *Journal of Personality and Social Psychology, 46,* 82–83.

Radebold, H. (1979). Der psychoanalytische Zugang zu dem älteren und alten Menschen [Psychoanalysis with elderly and old people]. In H. Petzold & E. Bubolz (Eds.), *Psychotherapie mit alten Menschen* (pp. 89–108). Paderborn: Jungfermann.

Ransen, D. L. (1978). Some determinants of decline among the institutionalized aged: Overcare. *Cornell Journal of Social Relations, 13,* 61–74.

Raps, C. S., Peterson, C., Jonas, M., & Seligman, M. E. P. (1982). Patient behavior in hospitals: Helplessness, reactance, or both? *Journal of Personality and Social Psychology, 42,* 1036–1041.

Regnier, V. (1981). *The neighborhood environment and its impact on the older person. Adaptability and aging.* Vol. 2. Paris: International Center for Social Gerontology.

Reichert, M. (1993). *Hilfeverhalten gegenüber alten Menschen: Eine experimentelle Überprüfung der Rolle von Erwartungen* [Helping behavior toward elderly people: An experimental analysis of expectations]. Essen: Blaue Eule.

Rodin, J., & Langer, E. J. (1977). Long-term effects of a control-relevant intervention with the institutionalized aged. *Journal of Personality and Social Psychology, 35,* 897–902.

Rosenmayr, L. (1983a). *Das Alter – Ein Stück bewusst gelebten Lebens* [Old age – a time of conscious living]. Berlin: Severin & Siedler.

   (1983b). *Die späte Freiheit* [The late freedom]. Berlin: Severin & Siedler.

Rothbaum, F., Weisz, J. R., & Snyder, G. G. (1982). Changing the world and changing the self: A two-process model of perceived control. *Journal of Personality and Social Psychology, 42,* 5–37.

Ryan, R. M., & Lynch, J. H. (1989). Emotional autonomy versus detachment: Revisiting the vicissitudes of adolescence and young adulthood. *Child Development, 60,* 340–356.

Sackett, G. P., Holm, R., Crowley, C., & Henkins, A. (1979). Computer technology: A Fortran program for lag sequential analysis of contingency and cyclicity in behavioral interaction data. *Behavior Research Methods and Instrumentation, 11,* 366–378.

Sampson, E. E. (1985). The decentralization of identity: Toward a revised concept of personal and social order. *American Psychologist, 40,* 1203–1211.

Sandholzer, H. (1982). Measuring impairment and disability in the elderly: A study in general practice. *Social Psychiatry, 17,* 189–198.

Schaffer, H. R., & Emerson, P. E. (1964). *The development of social attachments in infancy.* Monographie Social Research on Children Development, 29 (Special issue).

Schmid-Furstoss, U. (1990). *Subjektive Theorien von Unselbständigkeit und Selbständigkeit bei Seniorinnen aus Lebensumwelten mit unterschiedlichen Autonomieanforderungen* [Naive theories of dependence and independence held by the elderly from different ecologies]. Münster: Lit-Verlag, Psychologie 17.

Schulz, R. (1986). Successful aging: Balancing primary and secondary control. *Adult Development and Aging News, 13,* 2–4.

Schulz, R., Heckhausen, J., & Locher, J. L. (1992). Coping with problems related to health and aging: Matching control strategies with developmental trajectories. *Journal of Social Issues, 47,* 177–196.

Sears, R. R. (1972). Attachment, dependency, and frustration. In J. L. Gewirtz (Ed.), *Attachment and dependency* (pp. 1–27). New York: Wiley.

Sears, R. R., Maccoby, E. E., & Levin, H. (1957). *Patterns of childrearing.* Evanston, Ill.: Row, Petersen.

Sears, R. R., Rau, L., & Alpert, R. (1965). *Identification and childrearing.* Stanford, Calif.: Stanford University Press.

Sears, R. R., Whiting, J. W., Nowlis, V., & Sears, P. S. (1953). Some child-rearing antecedents of dependency and aggression in young children. *Genetic Psychology Monographs, 47,* 135–234.

Seligman, M. E. P. (1975). *Helplessness: On depression, development, and death.* San Francisco: W. H. Freemann & Co.

Shanas, E. P., Townsend, P., Wederburn, D., Friis, H., Miloj, J., & Stehouwer, J. (Eds.). (1968). *Old people in three industrial societies.* New York: Atherton Press.

Skinner, B. F. (1983). Intellectual self-management in old age. *American Psychologist, 38,* 239–244.

Skinner, E. A. (1985). Action, control judgment, and the structure of control experience. *Psychological Review, 92,* 39–58.

Skinner, E. A., & Connell, J. P. (1986). Control understanding: Suggestions for a developmental framework. In M. M. Baltes & P. B. Baltes (Eds.), *The psychology of control and aging* (pp. 35–70). Hillsdale, N.J.: Erlbaum.

Sosna, U., & Wahl, H.-W. (1983). Soziale Belastung, psychische Erkrankung und körperliche Beeinträchtigung im Alter: Ergebnisse einer Felduntersuchung [Social burden, mental and physical pathology in old age: An epidemiological study]. *Zeitschrift für Gerontologie, 16,* 107–114.

Spence, J. (1985). Achievement American style: The rewards and costs of individualism. *American Psychologist, 40,* 1285–1295.

Sperbeck, D. J., & Whitbourne, S. K. (1981). Dependency in the institutional setting: A behavioral training program for geriatric staff. *The Gerontologist, 21,* 268–275.

Sroufe, L. A., Fox, N. E., & Pancake, V. R. (1983). Attachment and dependency in developmental perspective. *Child Development, 54,* 1615–1627.

Sroufe, L. A., & Waters, E. (1977). Attachment as an organizational construct. *Child Development, 48,* 1184–1199.

Steinberg, L. (1990). Autonomy, conflict, and harmony in the family relationship. In S. Feldman & G. Elliot (Eds.), *At the threshold: The developing adolescent* (pp. 255–276). Cambridge, Mass.: Harvard University Press.

Steinberg, L., & Silverberg, S. (1986). The vicissitudes of autonomy in adolescence. *Child Development, 57,* 841–851.

Svanborg, A., Landahl, S., & Mehlström, D. (1982). Basic issues of health care. In H. Thomas & G. Maddox (Eds.), *New perspectives on old age* (pp. 31–52). New York: Springer.

Townsend, P. (1981). The structured dependency of the elderly: A creation of social policy in the twentieth century. *Aging and Society, 1,* 5–28.

van den Heuvel, W. (1976). The meaning of dependency. In J. M. A. Munnichs & W. van den Heuvel (Eds.), *Dependency or interdependency in old age* (pp. 162–173). The Hague, Netherlands: Martinus Nijhoff.

Verbrugge, L. M. (1989). Gender, aging, and health. In K. S. Markides (Ed.), *Aging and health: Perspectives on gender, race, ethnicity, and class* (pp. 23–78). Newbury Park, Calif.: Sage.

Wahl, H.-W. (1987). Behinderung in der Altenbevölkerung: Ergebnisse einer Feldstudie [Impairment in the aged population: Results of a field study]. *Zeitschrift für Gerontologie, 20,* 66–73.

    (1991). Dependence in the elderly from an interactional point of view: Verbal and observational data. *Psychology and Aging, 6,* 238–246.

    (1993). Kompetenzeinbussen im Alter: Eine Auswertung der Literatur zu "Activities of Daily Living" und Pflegebedürftigkeit [Competence loss in old age: An analysis of the literature on "Activities of Daily Living" and basic care needs]. *Zeitschrift für Gerontologie, 26,* 366–377.

Wahl, H.-W., & Baltes, M. M. (1990). Die soziale Welt pflegebedürftiger alter Menschen in Privathaushalten: Eine Beobachtungsstudie [The social world of older persons cared for in private households: An observational study]. *Zeitschrift für Entwicklungspsychologie und Pädagogische Psychologie, 22,* 266–283.

(1992). Die Mikroökologie alter Menschen: Forderung nach Autonomie und Sicherheit. In C. Petzold & H. G. Petzold (Eds.), *Die Lebenswelten alter Menschen* (pp. 96–119). Hannover: Vincentz Verlag.

Walker, A. (1980). The social creation of poverty and dependency in old age. *Journal of Social Policy, 9,* 172–188.

Wan, T. T. H., Odell, B. G., & Lewis, D. T. (1982). *Promoting the well-being of the elderly: A community diagnosis.* New York: Haworth Press.

Wisocki, P. (1984). Behavioral modification in the elderly. In M. Hersen, R. M. Eisler, & P. Miller (Eds.), *Progress in behavior modification,* Vol. 16 (pp. 121–158). New York: Academic Press.

World Health Organization. (1980). *International classification of impairments, disabilities, and handicaps.* Geneva: WHO.

Wortis, J. (1954). *Fragments of an analysis with Sigmund Freud.* New York: Simon & Schuster.

Zarit, S. H., Johansson, B., & Berg, S. (1993). Functional impairment and co-disability in the oldest-old: A multidimensional approach. *Journal of Aging and Health, 5,* 291–305.

Author Index

Subject Index